Partnering for Science: Proceedings of the U.S. Geological Survey Workshop on Citizen Science

Denver, Colorado
September 11–13, 2012

By Megan Hines, Abigail Benson, David Govoni, Derek Masaki, Barbara Poore, Annie Simpson, and Steven Tessler

Open-File Report 2013–1234

U.S. Department of the Interior
U.S. Geological Survey

U.S. Department of the Interior
SALLY JEWELL, Secretary

U.S. Geological Survey
Suzette M. Kimball, Acting Director

U.S. Geological Survey, Reston, Virginia: 2013

For more information on the USGS—the Federal source for science about the Earth, its natural and living resources, natural hazards, and the environment, visit http://www.usgs.gov or call 1–888–ASK–USGS.

For an overview of USGS information products, including maps, imagery, and publications,
visit http://www.usgs.gov/pubprod

To order this and other USGS information products, visit http://store.usgs.gov

Suggested citation:
Hines, Megan, Benson, Abigail, Govoni, David, Masaki, Derek, Poore, Barbara, Simpson, Annie, and Tessler, Steven, 2013, Partnering for Science; Proceedings of the USGS Workshop on Citizen Science: U.S. Geological Survey Open-File Report 2013–1234, 51 p., http://pubs.usgs.gov/of/2013/1234 .

Contents

Figure

Acknowledgments

The Citizen Science Workshop organizers (Abigail Benson, David Govoni, Megan Hines, Derek Masaki, Barbara Poore, Annie Simpson, and Steven Tessler) would like to thank the Community for Data Integration (CDI) and its executive sponsors for their support for our proposal and our working group's activities, which made the workshop possible. Other working group or CDI members whose input and support were crucial in planning and carrying out the event include: Sally Holl, Kelly Lotts, and Jake Weltzin. For their incredible patience and assistance with administrative logistics, planning, and travel support for the workshop, special thanks goes to Jennifer Carlino, Cheryl Davis, Sarah Davis, Terry D'Erchia, Cheryl Morris, Elizabeth Sellers, and Sarah Stephens. Finally, the workshop organizers would like to thank all of the invited speakers and attendees for their presentations and meaningful contributions to discussions at the event.

Community for Data Integration

The U.S. Geological Survey (USGS) CDI was established in 2009 to address data and information management issues affecting the proficiency of earth science research. The CDI provides a forum for collaboration and brainstorming by bringing together expertise from external partners and representatives across the USGS who are involved in research, data management, and information technology. Through partnerships and working groups, the CDI leads the development of data management tools and practices, cyberinfrastructure, collaboration tools, and training in support of scientists and technology specialists throughout the project life cycle. The CDI represents a dynamic community of practice focused on advancing science data and information management and integration capabilities across the USGS.

Foreword

The U.S. Geological Survey (USGS) Citizen Science Workshop, sponsored by the Community for Data Integration (CDI), brought together a dynamic group of professionals from six USGS mission areas and nine external experts who engage with citizens to achieve leading-edge science. These citizen science projects enable the USGS to showcase our assets, work collaboratively, improve our relevancy in the public eye, and actively engage citizens in science.

CDI has helped foster a new community of practice centered on citizen science; however, citizen science is not a new concept. From bird banding to the Audubon Society's Breeding Bird Survey and from The Voyage of The Beagle to amateur weather stations, the citizen science community has been a key contingent in data collection efforts for hundreds of years. Recently, citizen science has experienced a notable resurgence, with ideas such as Web 2.0, social networking, and broadly available, inexpensive data collection devices, including mobile smartphones.

While not new, citizen science has the ability to:

- make our USGS mission part of community life,
- engage the citizenry in learning about and contributing to science that expands our monitoring and data collection capability, and
- increase public understanding about what we do.

The results of the Citizen Science Workshop, coupled with ongoing CDI citizen science activities, provide an outstanding example of how CDI advances science data and information integration capabilities across the USGS. CDI objectives include promoting

Bureau-wide data integration, leading and participating in the development of a data management strategy for the USGS, and providing recommendations for implementation of data integration guidelines at the Bureau level.

Our commitment to the USGS citizen science community of practice is to foster success by investing in staff support, providing funding to help achieve stated goals, and advancing policy changes at the executive level to simplify and demystify the process of interacting with the public.

These proceedings from the first CDI Citizen Science Workshop corroborate and document the power that citizen science has to engage people at a fundamental level, leading to better science through incorporation of contributions by an active and engaged citizenry. Working across the spectrum of citizen scientists allows the USGS to leverage the public passion for science in achieving high-level mission goals.

We hope that you will consider participating with the CDI community in this and other exciting USGS science activities.

Kevin T. Gallagher, Associate Director for Core Science Systems

Linda C. Gundersen, Director, Office of Science Quality and Integrity (Emeritus)

Executive Summary

What U.S. Geological Survey (USGS) programs use citizen science? How can projects be best designed while meeting policy requirements? What are the most effective volunteer recruitment methods? What data should be collected to ensure validation and how should data be stored? What standard protocols are most easily used by volunteers? Can data from multiple projects be integrated to support new research or existing science questions? To help answer these and other questions, the USGS Community for Data Integration (CDI) supported the development of the Citizen Science Working Group (CSWG) in August 2011 and funded the working group's proposal to hold a USGS Citizen Science Workshop in fiscal year 2012.

The stated goals for our workshop were:

- raise awareness of programs and projects in the USGS that incorporate citizen science,

- create a community of practice for the sharing of knowledge and experiences,

- provide a forum to discuss the challenges of—and opportunities for—incorporating citizen science into USGS projects, and

- educate and support scientists and managers whose projects may benefit from public participation in science.

To meet these goals, the workshop brought together 50 attendees (see appendix A for participant details) representing the USGS, partners, and external citizen science practitioners from diverse backgrounds (including scientists, managers, project coordinators, and technical developers, for example) to discuss these topics at the Denver Federal Center in Colorado on September 11–12, 2012. Over two and a half days, attendees participated in four major plenary sessions (Citizen Science Policy and Challenges, Engaging the Public in Scientific Research, Data Collection and Management, and Technology and Tools) comprised of 25 invited presentations and followed by structured discussions for each session designed to address both prepared and ad hoc "big questions." A number of important community support and infrastructure needs were identified from the sessions and discussions, and a subteam was formed to draft a strategic vision statement to guide and prioritize future USGS efforts to support the citizen science community. Attendees also brainstormed proposal ideas for the fiscal year 2013 CDI request for proposals: one possible venue to support the execution of the vision.

Background

Origins of Citizen Science

The avocational engagement of interested individuals in scientific observation and research is not new. Amateur ornithologists monitored the timing of bird migration in 18th century Finland; in Victorian England, citizen astronomers participated in the British government's Transit of Venus project to accurately measure the distance from the Earth to the sun (Dickinson and others, 2010). In the United States, the Audubon Society's Christmas Bird Count (CBC) began in 1900 and has yielded long records of North American bird distribution; USGS volunteers have monitored the CBC "Brooke Circle" in Virginia continuously since 1947.

Indeed, it can be argued that the foundations of the formal academic physical and natural science disciplines in which the professional science establishment has operated since the late 19th century were laid by individuals like Benjamin Franklin, Charles Darwin, Charles Lyell, and many others stretching back into antiquity for whom science, or at least careful, systematic observation and recording of natural phenomena, was a passion not a career (Miller-Rushing and others, 2012; Silvertown, 2009).

Citizen Science Today

In recent years, the Internet, smartphones, and social media have revolutionized the way data can be collected by interested individuals and shared with scientists and researchers, resulting in a proliferation of formal and informal volunteer-supported science projects. Moreover, these technologies and channels of communication between citizens and scientists have spurred broader public interest, eased recruitment of volunteers, and allowed for increasingly sophisticated observation, monitoring, and other tasks to be carried out reliably and efficiently on a broad national and even global scale.

Recognition of the variety and scope of nonprofessional participation in all aspects of science has resulted in the evolution of the term "citizen science"—from a label used to describe projects in which nonspecialist volunteers collect observations and measurements or perform computations for use in science projects (Trumbull and others, 2000) to a more expansive and sophisticated concept of citizen science known as "the systematic collection and analysis of data; development of technology; testing of natural phenomena; and the dissemination of these activities by researchers on a primarily avocational basis." "Citizen scientist" is a "researcher who participates in the systematic collection and analysis of data; development of technology; testing of natural phenomena; and the dissemination of these activities on an avocational basis" (OpenScientist, written blog commun., 2011, accessed September 3, 2011, at *http://www.openscientist.org/2011/09/finalizing-definition-of-citizen.html*.) The term "citizen science" is being increasingly supplanted in the academic community by the more formal term "public participation in scientific research" (PPSR) (see Bonney and others, 2009; Shirk and others, 2012).

Consideration of the variety of relationships and division of responsibilities observed between professional and nonprofessional participants in citizen science-supported projects has led to the recognition of five models of public participation in scientific research based on factors, including level of participation in experimental design, contribution of observations, execution of data collection tasks, conduct of data analysis, dissemination of results, and so forth (Bonney and others, 2009; Shirk and others, 2012). The five models of public participation are as follows:

1. **Contractual projects**, where communities ask professional researchers to conduct a specific scientific investigation and report on the results;

2. **Contributory projects**, which are generally designed by scientists and for which members of the public primarily contribute data;

3. **Collaborative projects**, which are generally designed by scientists and for which members of the public contribute data but also help to refine project design, analyze data, and (or) disseminate findings;

4. **Co-created projects**, which are designed by scientists and members of the public working together and for which at least some of the public participants are actively involved in most or all aspects of the research process; and

5. **Collegial contributions**, where noncredentialed individuals conduct research independently with varying degrees of expected recognition by institutionalized science and (or) professionals.

Benefits and Value of Citizen Science

Citizen science is flourishing, in part because the volunteers and their professional counterparts perceive both short-term benefits and long-term value in their relationship (Duke, 2012).

For the Professional Researcher

The engagement of citizen scientists is increasingly viewed as a critical means of extending the reach of the science community "on the landscape," particularly where there are insufficient staff resources to generate the baseline and ongoing monitoring and other data required to address complex scientific issues because such activities are expensive, labor intensive, and time consuming (Duke, 2012; Lee and others, 2006; Silvertown, 2009).

For the Citizen Scientist

While perhaps harder to quantify, the benefits that accrue to citizen scientists are just as compelling. These include basic enjoyment in the study of nature, sense of community, interest and pride in contributing to the solution of an important local problem or in generally advancing scientific knowledge, interest in learning about the scientific process, and acquiring new skills (Duke, 2012).

For Society at Large

Citizen science, especially when consciously designed to engage students and teachers and when communicated to the general public, is also recognized as an important tool for promoting scientific literacy and understanding of scientific methods, improving analytic and other scientific skills, and generally improving relations between scientists and the general public (Bonney and others, 2009; Duke 2012).

Challenges and Concerns

The effective and reliable engagement of citizen scientists in any program of research, and in those of government institutions like the USGS in particular, generally is not without challenges and concerns.

Scientific Challenges

Scientific challenges center primarily on the question of trust in the quality of citizen-supplied data. While questions have been raised about the accuracy of citizen science data, research is beginning to show that properly designed, constrained, and managed citizen science can produce data that compare favorably to, and in some cases are superior to, authoritative data acquired by professional researchers (Catlin-Groves, 2012; Droege, 2007; Haklay, 2010).

Institutional Challenges

Practical concerns, including questions of liability for injury, protection of privacy, level of access to government computer systems and data, and the implications of access to or contact with rare, endangered, or dangerous organisms, may prevent or severely limit the effective employment of citizen scientists in USGS research programs. Scientists wishing to "do the right thing" and meet all the necessary requirements for the legal and ethical use of citizen scientists' time and data are confronted with a myriad of complex, often outdated, and sometimes contradictory regulations pertaining to the employment of volunteers.

Federal research focus on big national concerns rather than on the kinds of local issues most likely to spark citizen enthusiasm and engagement may inhibit volunteer recruiting. Uneven or unreliable postkickoff funding to assure long-term research project viability, though not unique to citizen science-oriented projects, may impact them by devaluing results and discouraging volunteer retention.

Other constraints imposed on Federal application developers relating to government-commercial sector contractual relationships (for example, Terms of Service (TOS) agreements for software application deployment) have often proven to be significant impediments to distributing and making effective use of modern tools, such as simple smartphone-based data collection applications.

Citizen Science in the USGS

The USGS conducts or supports several well-known, long-term, and very large-scale citizen science efforts organizing volunteers to provide needed observations and baseline information to support its science. The North American Breeding Bird Survey program provides status and trend information about bird populations across the continent. Another program, the USA National Phenology Network, brings together volunteer citizen scientists, government agencies, nonprofit groups, educators, and students of all ages in monitoring the life cycles of animals and plants, providing valuable phenological data for climate change research in the United States (Schwartz and others, 2012; Weltzin, 2011). The "Did You Feel It?" system collects and processes citizen-supplied reports of earthquake shaking and damage to rapidly generate and communicate regional macroseismic intensity maps (Wald and others, 2011). The USGS Nonindigenous Aquatic Species (NAS) is one of the oldest Web-based USGS databases and receives reports of species occurrences from both scientists and the public through a Web-reporting form, via email, and by telephone. These and other citizen science-supported projects currently underway within the USGS, including those highlighted in this workshop's presentations, posters, and other resources (appendixes B, C, E, and G) generally fall within the "Contributory" class of PPSR project—those designed by scientists and involving volunteers to collect samples and (or) data.

Community Development, Collaboration, and Support for USGS Citizen Science

Computer and information sciences play an increasingly important role in supporting and furthering the USGS mission in earth systems science monitoring and research (U.S. Geological Survey, 2007). To better meet the data acquisition, processing, analysis, sharing, and management needs of its scientists, the USGS has formed the Core Science Systems (CSS) mission area, which sponsors the CDI and manages the Applied Earth Systems Informatics Research (AESIR) program.

The CSWG is an interdisciplinary and interagency team within the CDI that focuses on building a community of practice for public participation in USGS science. The CSWG has four overarching goals:

- promote an understanding of the role and potential benefits of citizen science and scientists in the conduct of the USGS mission;

- facilitate and enhance connections between the USGS and the citizen science community;

- provide access to information and tools to support the proper, effective, and creative use of citizen science data inside and outside the USGS; and

- engage the public in USGS and partner science and improve scientific literacy.

The CSWG collaborates with researchers and technologists from AESIR, other CDI working groups, and partner agencies and organizations, such as universities to advance the use of citizen science as an integral and valued component of USGS programs. Through CSWG working group activities like this workshop, the development of informational Web sites, and more formal research and development efforts, such as the creation and deployment of mobile data collection applications, the CDI and AESIR are striving to deliver advanced infrastructure, tools, and methods to USGS scientists already engaged in, or considering, citizen-supported science.

The following session summaries are organized in the order they were presented at the workshop. The format for each summary, with the exception of the opening session, includes a brief introduction describing why the session topic is of interest, followed by an overview of each presentation delivered. The introduction and overview are followed by highlights from the session's facilitated discussion, and closes with suggestions and observations heard in the sessions from participants for best practices on each session topic. Detailed appendices include additional artifacts from the workshop, including: a participant list, full abstracts for presentations and posters, a detailed agenda, copies of or references to meeting handouts provided by attendees, useful resources on volunteer monitoring, a detailed list of citizen science activities, as well as a glossary that explains abbreviations and terms from the text. Hyperlinks and external references are provided to supplement the information presented. The links were last checked on June 24, 2013.

Session Summary: Opening and Welcome

The opening session of our workshop provided an opportunity for our regional hosts and our executive sponsor to welcome participants to our workshop, as well as set the stage for our four main sessions.

Welcome

Megan Hines, cochair of the CSWG, welcomed in-room and virtual attendees to the USGS Citizen Science Workshop, as well as shared a brief set of logistics to the group in the room in Denver.

Randy Updike, USGS Regional Executive for the Rocky Mountain Area, welcomed workshop participants to Denver and commented on citizen science-related initiatives in which he has been involved. He highlighted local community knowledge as a key component of success for the projects. Technology advances are expanding the interface with the public, and Randy is excited to see how these advances can support the science.

Linda Gundersen, USGS Director of the Office of Science Quality and Integrity and CDI Executive Sponsor, welcomed everyone and shared her joint excitement with the attendees on the topics of crowdsourcing and citizen science. She has been involved in many up-and-coming initiatives that are seeking to expand USGS involvement in the realm of science education. Linda suggested we ask ourselves what we could do with all the citizens around the globe. How can we engage the millions of students excited about science? How can we involve citizens in research to improve our science? Can USGS spread scientific literacy and tap into observational efforts and facilitate data collection and aggregation? Kevin Gallagher and Linda Gundersen began working on an upcoming competition to provide funds to USGS scientists working with citizen scientists and groups, such as local and State nature societies, schools, and others.

Jennifer Shirk provided an opening presentation offering strategic direction suggestions. Her presentation included supporting success stories and positive outcomes from the broader community of research to serve as motivation for our attendees.

Jennifer gave great suggestions to our audience on how we as an agency, as individuals through our own efforts, and as a part of the larger citizen science research community should look for collaboration opportunities and make investments in projects where citizen science engagement provides for positive benefits across science, education, and society.

By providing and engaging in meaningful experiences with the public in places in which they have a stake in and cherish, they are motivated to engage in efforts to protect their local treasures and areas of interest.

Session Summary: Policy and Challenges

Introduction

How does the USGS and the Department of the Interior (DOI) policy affect our citizen science projects today? What do we need to know to comply with these policies? What are the challenges that USGS scientists face when setting up citizen science projects? This session outlined compelling policy issues and other challenges related to mobile application development, the USGS volunteer program, the management of personally identifiable information (PII), and the Paperwork Reduction Act (PRA).

The "Policy & Challenges" session, facilitated by Annie Simpson, was intended to both clarify USGS and Federal Government policies and provide a platform for citizen science researchers to share instances of where policy has not worked well for them. Often these issues have become cases of "lessons learned" and were shared for the common good. In the future, through collaboration with the USGS, volunteers may be asking the big scientific questions. Presentations were given by participants both in the room and via WebEx.

Summary of Presentations

Lorna Schmid opened the session by discussing the USGS Mobile Framework, which (like the Citizen Science Workshop) is a CDI-funded project for 2012. The goal of the framework is to provide all pertinent information for the lifecycle of mobile application development, including workflows that outline the steps for developing, testing, publishing, and monitoring applications. Steps in the workflows ensure that appropriate policies applicable to all areas are addressed.

There is a strong need for a mobile application community that can provide mutual support, collaboration, peer reviews, vetting of ideas, have training in application development, and share lessons learned across its members. This is especially true because mobile development involves multiple challenges; technology is rapidly changing; there is a need to avoid duplicated efforts; and it is important to collaborate on common tools. For fiscal year 2013, the group is developing a new proposal to expand their community site. The goals are to enhance collaboration, improve workflow tracking, develop tools, and hold town-hall meetings to get input from science centers and others.

Robert Thieler described some of his research that studies Piping Plovers, an endangered shorebird species that nests in low-lying areas affected by storm surges, overwash (water and sediment left behind when water levels are above normal), and sea-level rise. In order to monitor the population, nesting, and movement of these birds, he developed a smartphone application for trained Piping Plover biologists to utilize. Ownership of smartphones is widespread among Rob's peers. It seems natural to use smartphones in the collection of timely data to aid rapid decisionmaking information needs.

Rob found that while collecting useful data is readily achievable using mobile tools, just because folks have smartphones does not necessarily mean they know how to use them. In addition, daunting policy issues, such as guidance for mobile applications, privacy, PII, iconography, branding, openID, and Office of Management and Budget (OMB) approval are some expected hurdles on the path to success for deploying a mobile application (app). It would be helpful to have agency-level blanket permits to address the PRA and TOS issues.

Cheryl Smith described the traditional approach to volunteer engagement in USGS citizen science found in the Volunteer for Science Handbook. For individuals planning to volunteer for more than 180 days, some examples of the requirements for volunteering include:

- being fingerprinted;

- obtaining a photo identification;

- obtaining National Agency Check with Inquiries (NACI) clearance if there is a need to use a computer on the USGS network;

- signing release forms protecting the USGS from claims of injury, death, or loss of property; and

- attending training on scientific integrity.

The Volunteer for Science Handbook also describes the roles and steps to become an emeritus scientist, who is officially a volunteer who can complete scientific investigations, mentor, serve on committees, and perform other activities at the USGS. Cheryl also described the Federal Interagency Team on Volunteerism, which promotes national leadership and coordination, offers support on education, and trains regarding the development and maintenance of volunteer positions. Cheryl suggested USGS scientists use the Volunteer.gov Web site to recruit volunteers. The USGS Human Resources would like to market the volunteer program more broadly to make it more approachable.

Eric Wolf and **Barbara Poore** gave a team presentation on volunteerism in scientific research from a USGS researcher's point of view. Currently, USGS volunteers are required to follow multiple requirements in order to participate in USGS activities, and programs must address multiple policy and information collection clearance requirements before information collection can begin. Eric pointed out that even though the USGS Volunteer Handbook covers extensive activities required for volunteering and even firearm safety, it does not cover the most common situations, such as children participating as part of a classroom project. Is parental approval required? Can the teacher act as a monitor and submit class data to the USGS? What about people voluntarily submitting data from their own computers when they never leave their home? Do they all need to be validated as official USGS volunteers? Although citizen science is inherently global, the current handbook states volunteers must be U.S. citizens or have a green card. We would like to see significant expansion to the handbook to provide broader guidance for initiators of citizen science projects.

Shari Baloch and **David Newman** shared their expertise on PRA, the Privacy Act and PII, and the Freedom of Information Act (FOIA) and how they relate to launching citizen science programs. The PRA requires agencies to acquire OMB approval before collecting structured information from 10 or more members of the public per year. This includes any focus groups, administering forms or Web-page surveys, as well as mobile apps that collect information. OMB approval of the use of questionnaires with the public can be a lengthy process. If you know of any unapproved efforts underway, let Shari know so she can help them gain approval rather than be discovered after the fact. All USGS records are subject to FOIA, as is any data collected by our citizen scientists. All of us are all responsible for protecting PII, which means a privacy impact assessment (PIA) must be conducted before this kind of information can be collected. A handout Shari produced for the workshop is available in appendix E to help you determine when to get assistance in this area.

Paul Earle spoke on behalf of Sophia Liu about the Tweet Earthquake Dispatch (TED), which uses geospatial crowdsourcing to detect major seismic events through ongoing real-time computer analysis of Twitter feeds for earthquake terms in several languages. TED started in 2009 after a large earthquake in China killed 60,000–70,000 people and bloggers claimed that Twitter users knew about the earthquake before the USGS did. Access to Twitter was blocked behind the USGS firewall at that time, so private off-site research was required. Paul wrote a short paper that showed the potential ways to use the Twitter data in earthquake detection and since the speed of sound (speed of earthquakes) takes longer to travel than the speed of light (Twitter), and earthquake sensors are not everywhere, this method of detecting earthquakes is highly successful. TED now detects earthquakes in as little as 18 seconds.

Matt Cannister described the NAS database's online reporting tool, which had significant hurdles for OMB approval. The NAS contains 80,000 occurrence records for 950+ nonnative freshwater species, and each record shows 20–30 data fields. New occurrences, as they are verified, feed into a subscription alerts system and enable subscribers to perform rapid responses to new invasions. The NAS has also developed with USGS partners an online sighting report form as a mobile app. While the development was easy to do and is based on a questionnaire with previous OMB approval, it has not been deployed because the USGS is waiting for DOI to approve a comprehensive process for app development and TOS for distribution.

Facilitated Discussion Highlights

The following topics were discussed after the presentations:

- Digital Strategy: Every government agency has to announce public digital applications, and DOI has made that part of its digital strategy (*http://www.doi.gov/digitalstrategy/index.cfm*), although it is a work in process.

- PRA: If USGS Citizen Science projects have Web forms to collect data that are approved and the mobile app is the same, additional OMB approval as specified by the PRA is not required. For new requests, the OMB fast track system has a 3-week turnaround. It used to take up to 2 years.

- TOS for mobile app development: The TOS contract required for iPhone app development is a legal requirement at the DOI level and it is also a current roadblock. The National Phenology Network is also currently going through the process for a 3-year approval of their app that was developed by their university partners.

- Partnerships: We need to sort out policy issues to maintain our credentials and funding. There is a strong need to highlight the excellence of the USGS and our efforts. We should focus on dreams and what can be done. The Mobile Framework will help address the technical, development, and policy aspects. Long-term monitoring and data collection need more stability and long-term involvement than the private sector (that is, universities) can provide alone; still, the USGS should partner with those who can help.

- Describe our needs for USGS leadership: The building of an app is a very quick process. It is the approval process that is cumbersome. There is a need to foster our grassroots efforts like TED, iPlover, and NAS, and having an overarching vision and strategic plan will help. We will establish the big questions we want to answer, describe how we will work together, the kinds of communities we will form, and the issues that the USGS leadership needs to address.

- Understanding PII: Scientists organizing citizen science projects may not understand the requirements concerning PII, and the lay public may be unaware of any potential issue with sharing their information. A name alone is not PII. Whenever two or more pieces of PII connect together, there is a concern. TED uses one-way encryption on a user name to avoid PII violations.

- Policy guideline resources: For those who want to learn more about policy guidelines and regulations, the Office of Science and Technology Policy (OSTP) Web site is a great place to find many of them, but others are scattered widely. The group determined that it would be useful to have a USGS resource that helps sort them.

Observations and Suggested Best Practices

Navigating DOI and USGS Policy

The USGS wants to endorse and continue participating in projects—showcasing them and providing support to compliant programs—and also wants to help existing noncompliant programs get through the hurdles to compliance. There are projects underway at the USGS that are developing draft solutions and spearheading efforts to break down multiple challenges that the workshop participants have concerns about relating to mobile application development, from ideation through publication.

Suggested best practice.—Project planning should include careful consideration of activities that need USGS policy/area approvals, and principal investigators must ensure these requirements are met soon after conception, so that USGS participation in the project is legal and activities to gather information to advance our science can continue.

Suggested best practice.—If any policies augment or shape your project, be transparent about the policies with volunteers. Let them know why you are doing something a certain way or what policies apply.

There are several USGS scientists and policy specialists investigating if there is a way to shorten OMB approval-time turn-around, and possibly organize a blanket approval or group approval of several existing applications-in-waiting. The time length for approval can go very quickly or can be lengthy. Many groups are unsure where they are in the process or even if it applies to their project. All project managers should work with the USGS Information Collection Officer and USGS Privacy Officer to get their projects into the appropriate approval queues for OMB approval and PIA, if necessary.

Suggested best practice.—The CSWG should create a decision tree for navigating policy and other Bureau or department requirements for launching citizen science programs. The purpose of the decision tree is to help navigate the policy requirements process for USGS scientists organizing citizen science projects. It should intersect with the mobile framework when mobile application development is a component of the program. Similar to the mobile framework, we should consider a rotating champion or ombudsperson to be a contact for citizen science program questions, who will work closely with Bureau policy personnel. An alternative to this approach is to provide this resource as a working group with appropriate support.

DOI Volunteer Program

A variety of support is available to volunteer programs through Cheryl Smith and the USGS Volunteer Program's activities. The USGS Volunteer Handbook provides information to everyone about involving a volunteer in USGS science. Updates or suggestions to the handbook are welcomed by Cheryl, who is Program Coordinator with the USGS Volunteer for Science Program. A suggestion was made that we ought to examine current policies to determine applicability and ask: "Are they old policies?" Do they need to be addressed and updated to reflect new White House initiatives, memoranda, and strategies? When conflicting guidance occurs, which one rules?

Suggested best practice.—The USGS should review and make any necessary revisions to the Volunteer for Science Handbook to assure that the recruitment process is as flexible and easy as possible.

Session Summary: Engaging the Public in Scientific Research

Introduction

Citizen scientists' participation in scientific research, whether as casual observers and recorders of natural phenomena or as full partners with professional scientists in the design and execution of experiments, is motivated and sustained by many factors. This session, cochaired by Barbara Poore and David Govoni, focused on how and why citizens participate in scientific projects. Presenters were drawn from citizen science projects that spanned a range of project types, topics, sponsoring organizations, scales, and geographies. Presenters and participants in the facilitated discussion that followed the talks were asked to consider and touch on the following questions:

- What motivates citizens to participate?

- How can projects be designed for the mutual benefit of scientists and citizens?

- What are effective techniques to engage, encourage, and retain volunteers?

- Are rewards effective? If so, what kinds of rewards?

- What different types of organizational structures, protocols, and user materials have proven effective?

- How can volunteer-dependent projects sustain themselves?

Summary of Presentations

Barbara Horn has years of experience managing different types of volunteer water-quality monitoring programs in Colorado. She described how volunteer water-quality monitoring began as an essentially local community education and stewardship activity but has evolved into a more formalized range of activities supporting State-level decisionmaking. In their expanded roles, volunteers are treated as a workforce and currently make up about one-third of the total State-wide monitoring personnel. The volunteers who work on projects for the National Water Quality Monitoring Council essentially do the same work as professionals.

The water-quality monitoring programs are tiered, based on how rigorous the standards are and on the complexity and amount of time that is involved to collect information. There are resource and data-availability issues with the tiered approach relating to the uneven availability of volunteers with sufficient background knowledge and skills necessary to master complex methods and sophisticated equipment to perform higher level tasks.

On the other hand, River Watch, which Barbara Horn has also managed, relies on uniform procedures requiring a common level of competence from its volunteers. Seven hundred sites are monitored each year. Tasks include fieldwork, laboratory analysis, physical habitat measurement, identifying macroinvertebrates, and taking photographs. Volunteers are trained, provided with necessary equipment, and must meet common quality standards in order to participate.

Volunteers are motivated to participate due to a variety of personal, and often local, concerns and interests (for example, impacts of water pollution on wildlife, potential risks to drinking water supplies due to fracking, and so forth). They are most engaged when they can see clear connections between their efforts and how their concerns are addressed.

Andrea Wiggins is a Postdoctoral Fellow at DataONE, a global project to apply cyberinfrastructure and big data analysis to environmental issues, and the Cornell University Lab of Ornithology, which has a long history of citizen participation in its research. Andrea discussed the range of interactions between citizen volunteers and scientists and the labels applied to them, preferring the more generic term "Public Participation in Scientific Research" (PPSR) to "citizen science." She noted that PPSR spans many research domains, including political science, ecology, natural resource management, behavioral science, psychology, and management.

The roles volunteers can play in these domains are varied and complex. They can be consultative (when scientists seek guidance about issues from stakeholders), functional (when volunteers collect data or perform other tasks), or collaborative (when there is mutual feedback about research questions, methods, goals, and interpretations among citizens and scientists). Models of direct citizen participation range from contribution (simple collection and analysis of samples) to collaboration (including research design and data analysis) and cocreation with scientists (including all phases of research, from defining the question through experiment design, interpretation, and dissemination of results). Andrea Wiggins and her colleagues have developed a typology (Shirk and others, 2012) to describe the various classes of PPSR based on research goals and scientific tasks performed. These models can guide scientists as they consider how best to engage citizen volunteers in their projects.

Factors to be considered within this typological framework include task complexity, necessary level of data quality and scalability, availability and suitability of supporting technologies, project resources and sustainability, and necessary level of volunteer management.

Andrea Wiggins recommended that scientists honestly evaluate their resources and goals and work backwards from there to ensure appropriate and effective use of volunteers. She stressed the need to recognize tradeoffs (for example, detailed, high-quality local data may not scale to a continental level), and to address resource and other constraints from the beginning and design the project accordingly (recognizing there is more than one approach to effective citizen engagement).

Greg Newman, an Ecologist/Web Designer at Colorado State University, described his research and work to provide infrastructure and communication tools for those who would like to organize and manage citizen science projects. His presentation began by asking what role cyberinfrastructure might play in supporting citizen science, given the sheer volume and variety of data that are being generated by the growing body of projects. He noted that teaching and participation are the essence of discovery and that PPSR projects need a mix of committed volunteers, scientists, and "mavens" (project coordinators or facilitators) to fulfill one of their major nonscientific social benefits—providing the impetus for sustained participation, learning, and personal enrichment in the sciences.

Established PPSR projects benefit from access to shared tools and infrastructure that encourage communication, collaboration, and knowledge sharing. One of his projects, CitSci.org, provides a framework to support the formation of new PPSR projects and to encourage effective collaboration among existing projects. Anyone, anywhere, can create a new project in this system. CitSci.org supports both citizen-driven and scientist-driven tools and methods that help with project creation, management of members, collection, analysis, interpretation, management of data, and sharing of results.

Greg demonstrated the Web site (*http://www.citsci.org*) and its functionalities. Since 2008, the Web site has supported more than 40 projects with hundreds of participants that have collected over 7,000 observations leading to many peer-reviewed publications. The collocated online project spaces help PPSR projects succeed by promoting shared practice, amplifying collective intelligence, and restructuring expert attention (ideas drawn from Nielsen, 2012).

Project leaders can motivate individual participants in a variety of ways, including sharing ownership, highlighting progress, encouraging regular feedback and dialogue, and through rewards. Effective rewards include direct acknowledgment or attribution as part of the communication of results, including coauthorship of scientific papers.

The CitSci.org community approach benefits participating projects by encouraging common practices and standards. In particular, the quality of data and value of results are enhanced across member communities through the adoption of shared vocabularies, common protocols, and the use of common, yet flexible, data collection, description, and other technical standards. The community approach also allows for individual expertise to be amplified for the benefit of all member communities through knowledge sharing. Knowledge-sharing approaches that have proven most effective over the range of projects in CitSci.org are Train the Trainer and crowdsourcing.

Greg Newman discussed plans for future site enhancements, including tools for event management, improved online training support, better volunteer tracking, customized reporting, and new social communication and marketing capabilities. Advanced informatics capabilities, including data exchange Application Programming Interfaces (APIs) and a mobile app for data collection, are also contemplated.

Greg Matthews, Project Manager for The National Map Corps, described past and present efforts to engage the public in volunteer map data collection at the USGS. Greg noted that volunteers have long been involved in various aspects of topographic mapping at the USGS through the years, but early attempts to collect citizen-supplied data online were suspended in 2004 due to budgetary constraints. A renewed program to enlist the support of volunteers to collect data for *The National Map*—the digital equivalent of the paper topographic map—was launched in 2011 and is being carried out in three phases.

The first phase of the project investigated whether open-source software used by OpenStreetMap, a map of the world generated by volunteers, could be repurposed to support collaborative editing of transportation data between the USGS and the Kansas Data Access and Support Center. The project proved that collaborative editing was possible, but that transportation data might be too complex or unsophisticated for volunteers to provide assistance. The second phase of the project shifted focus to the collection of structures data (points of interest) using the online mapping system. Student volunteers were recruited from GIS classes at Denver area universities to collect data on structures over four quadrangles covering metropolitan Denver. The project included Wikipedia-style editing by which students quality checked the data produced during editing. The USGS performed a detailed in-house quality-control assessment on each point, which demonstrated that student volunteers were capable of collecting data that met horizontal positional accuracy standards suitable for incorporation into The National Map. To assist students, there was an extensive online help manual. Students were recognized through certificates of achievement.

The third phase of the project is called The National Map Corps. In this phase, the same map interface is used from the second phase, but volunteers are asked to collect structures data for the entire State of Colorado. Anyone can volunteer. This phase also has an "Adopt-a-Quad" feature for checking other volunteers' contributions. Experienced editors can adopt and monitor the accuracy of contributions of others in a particular USGS quadrangle. From March to August 2012, over 1,400 edits had been made by volunteers.

Greg stressed the importance of constantly improving and simplifying the editing interface for volunteers and of providing comprehensive online training, including user guides and videos, to show volunteers how to properly submit and edit their contributions.

Kristi Wallace provided an overview and shared lessons learned about the Alaska Volcano Observatory's very successful engagement with citizen scientists in support of their volcanic ash observation and collection program. Because active volcanoes are remote from the observatory, and eruptions which cause ash fall are ephemeral and often of very broad aerial extent, public observations and voluntary collection and submission of ash-fall samples provide crucial contributions to the Alaska Volcano Observatory. Dispersal patterns reported by volunteers can help ground-truth satellite data and improve ash-fall models. Ash-fall collections can also aid in the development of isomass contour maps, showing the distribution of ash falls as lines of equal mass. Local people in widely distributed communities are ideally situated to collect good quality samples.

The documentation provided by observers varies widely. To assure that observations provided by the volunteer network are as complete, consistent, and accurate as possible, the project uses a variety of training methods, including the provision of simple and explicitly written visual guides, videos, and workshops. Key groups are cultivated as volunteers. There are different types of observations of varying sophistication that citizens can contribute, including eye witness accounts, measurements of thickness, and various types of direct sampling. Volunteers are encouraged to engage in only those tasks that they feel able to perform well. Information is collected via Web forms, but also through paper worksheets. A ruler printed on the side of a data collection sheet has been a key tool to help prevent guessing ash thickness. OMB approval is currently being sought for a new ash-fall reporting system and database. This system uses a structured questions format to lead volunteers through the data input process.

Data presented on the public-facing Web site are aggregated and stripped of PII to assure privacy. The information maintained in the program's internal data management system is much more detailed. The system is used to deliver observations to the National Weather Service for their "Ashfall Advisory Statements." Volunteer contact information is maintained to permit program staff to verify unusual or suspect observations or to conduct special observations. Provision of this contact information is strictly voluntary; observers may opt out and contribute their observations anonymously.

A great number of samples and observations are sent in for each eruption. Many of these are provided by contributors who have remained loyal to the program over the long term. Maximizing personal contact and letting people know that their contributions are appreciated have proven effective in cultivating these long-term relationships. For example, hand-written thank you notes with pictures of a particular eruption are sent to observers who provided ash samples. Another enticement to stay interested and involved in the program that has proven very successful is to encourage the public to contribute photographs for public display, with proper attribution, on the program's Web site.

Facilitated Discussion Highlights

The following topics were discussed after the presentations:

- Expansion and Reuse of Online Tools: The potential for better integrating data/metadata input and exchange between projects (for example, as is being done now for images shared between iNaturalist and Encyclopedia of Life (EOL))—an "input once, publish many" model for data acquisition—was discussed. Concern was raised about the flexibility of existing project platforms, like DiscoverLife and CitSci.org, in terms of their ability to mutually support such things as the use of common metadata models and data collection protocols.

- Common Protocols: Discussion of the need for simple yet flexible group protocols for data collection. Participants in existing and new projects should be encouraged to adopt common collection protocols to the maximum extent possible. Cornell is working on a directory of protocols and other reference materials.

- Volunteer Motivation: Is there concern among citizen science groups about citizens losing control of data? Barbara Horn and others noted that in their experience, letting go of the data was of less concern to volunteers than frustration (leading to loss of interest) when their data are not clearly used or acknowledged. Steve Tessler described his project to document his county's biodiversity. For him, copyright—specifically the issue of stealing and using photos put on the Web in violation of copyright—is a major concern. There has to be a clear understanding on the part of contributors of the implications of data and image sharing with projects (for example, the required use of one of the less restrictive "Attribution" Creative Commons licenses for photographs submitted to EOL). This led into a general discussion about why people volunteer to document future change.

- Education: The importance of leveraging opportunities afforded by citizen science projects to educate both student and nonstudent citizens in the principles and practice of science was stressed. This may prove difficult at the USGS. The Office of Education is minimally staffed and scientists are generally not given professional credit and are even discouraged from participating in educational outreach. We need greater engagement with students at all formal educational levels, from kindergarten through postgraduate, as well as with retirees and others engaged in life-long learning. Enhancing scientific literacy and generating excitement in the sciences is critical to recruiting the next generation of scientists.

- Value and Funding of Citizen Science: How to prove value of citizen science: It is difficult to get the National Science Foundation (NSF) to fund citizen science projects on scientific merit and application alone. (NSF would rather fund projects as part of national outreach or educational efforts like the Science, Technology, Engineering, and Math (STEM) initiatives). In the USGS, we need to show that for a variety of our activities, well-designed and carefully managed citizen science is a cost-effective way to generate quality data and supplements traditional methods in our science. The importance of involving the USGS programs (where the money is) and involving other agencies and partners in promoting and integrating citizen science was stressed.

Observations and Suggested Best Practices

Based on the presentations, discussions, and information shared, below are a number of best practices and considerations to note about the design, management, and sustainability efforts for projects.

Project Design, Management, and Support

When designing a citizen science project:

- Be realistic about project goals, resources, and constraints and engage citizen volunteers accordingly.

- Provide volunteers with clear instructions and the simplest tools necessary to make their tasks as easy to accomplish, and the results as consistent and accurate, as possible.

- Do not try to force volunteers to do things they do not feel comfortable doing. Give them the option to perform only those tasks that they feel competent to do well.

Organizers of citizen science projects should let the projects' goals and tasks dictate the project design (for example, collaborative, co-created, or contributory). The design must take into account factors such as scalability, technology availability or constraints, and level of available resources. Project design also influences how volunteers are best managed, the nature and complexity of tasks able to be performed, resultant data quality, and project sustainability.

To achieve high-quality observations from volunteers, data collection, submission, and related applications should be easy to use and developed based upon best design practices. These practices include the:

- employment of simple workflows,

- use of standardized forms and prompts,

- provision of drop-down pick lists of terms, and

- incorporation of error trapping and validation methods as data are collected and submitted.

Projects should also consider the demographics and other characteristics of their volunteers when making technology decisions. See appendix F for findings from a giving and charitable behavior study describing characteristics of participants.

In order to effectively utilize required processes and technology, training volunteers in the proper use of devices, applications, and techniques is a necessity.

Advancing the Field Together

Form and Expand Partnerships and Pilot Studies

Suggested best practice.—USGS researchers should seek opportunities to form or expand partnerships with external citizen science organizations and projects in order to advance the field of public participation in scientific research together.

Suggested best practice.—The USGS should leverage existing relationships to quickly organize and implement pilot projects aimed at both supporting our research and demonstrating the value of public participation in scientific research to the wider USGS research community.

Suggested best practice.—In developing these initial partnerships and pilot studies, the USGS should seek to create and cultivate strong, long-term links between citizen scientists and USGS science programs.

Leverage Existing Resources

USGS scientists contemplating designing a citizen-supported project have access to many examples of successful projects and community experiences in virtually every major field of science. These projects can be used as models to guide the development of our own projects and programs. There is no reason to "go it alone" or "reinvent the wheel." For example:

- Barbara Horn from Colorado Parks and Wildlife offered many suggestions for helpful resources to review on many aspects of program development and continuing engagement related to her years of experience with Colorado River Watch (*http://wildlife.state.co.us/LandWater/Riverwatch/Pages/Riverwatch.aspx*). See appendix F for access to some of these resources.

- The CitSci.org Web site has a list of existing data collection and measurement protocols available at *http://www.citsci.org/cwis438/websites/citsci/Standards.php?WebSiteID=7* that can be used or quickly modified for new projects.

- The Cornell Lab of Ornithology, through its Citizen Science Central portal (*http://www.birds.cornell.edu/citscitoolkit*), has developed a comprehensive and expanding resource for references and guides to project development, design, protocols, and more.

Workshop participants agreed that the USGS should consider how to make effective use of, contribute to, or collaborate in these groups' efforts.

Suggested best practice.—The CDI CSWG should take the lead in encouraging and coordinating information and knowledge exchange between the USGS and external citizen science community support organizations and facilities.

Suggested best practice.—The USGS should establish a "USGS Citizen Science" Web site and associated knowledge repository to collect, organize, and share project creation, management, and operational information. That information would include such things as a project inventory, data collection protocols, legal and other administrative guidelines and requirements, training materials, project design, available tools and technologies, and best practices.

Expand Internal Communication, Coordination, Collaboration, and Mutual Support

Suggested best practice.—The CDI CSWG and USGS citizen science project coordinators should work together to create sustainable relationships for the purpose of communication, coordination, collaboration, and mutual support.

Appendix G lists and describes USGS and non-USGS citizen science projects discussed during the workshop. USGS scientists considering the use of citizen scientists in support of their research are encouraged to engage in these projects to share ideas and best practices.

Support Science Education While Advancing Our Science

Suggested best practice.—The CDI CSWG should engage with other groups and programs across the USGS to develop a strategic vision and generate ideas for:

- encouraging USGS scientists and technologists to empower schools and communities nationwide to conduct or support meaningful local and national scientific surveys, and

- developing coordinated strategies to use citizen science as a vehicle for integrating our science into educational programs at all levels.

Communication and Outreach

In order to achieve broad exposure for projects and to celebrate their successes, information about the projects must be broadcast widely through all available venues, including the USGS Web site and mailing lists.

Suggested best practice.—The CDI CSWG should coordinate with USGS projects leads and the USGS Office of Communications and Publishing to systematically highlight and promote our citizen-supported research activities and opportunities. Methods could include periodic "Science Feature" stories, blog posts, interviews with project leads or participants, news releases, and so forth.

Suggested best practice.—The working group should expand its own internal outreach and information sharing activities by regularly providing opportunities for USGS and external scientists or groups to describe and discuss their citizen science projects. Opportunities include the group's regular meetings; CDI monthly meetings and, as appropriate, workshops; round table sessions; executive leadership briefings; or other venues.

Societal Impacts

Engaging volunteers in scientific activities provides an excellent opportunity to expand the reach and depth of our investigations while simultaneously exciting participants about USGS science. The use of citizen volunteers also provides direct societal benefits in the form of technology training and, most importantly, providing them with a deeper understanding of science principles and practice.

Investing in the local community by sharing science experiences with them directly, rather than bringing in scientists from elsewhere, to gather data or solve a problem provides valuable skills to local residents as they enter higher education or the job market. Engaging educators demonstrates the value of the volunteer experience as a direct benefit to students as well as a support and enhancement to the curriculum. Programs like Hawaii's STEMWorks and Discover Life's Mothing Project develop critical thinking skills in students, solve real problems in their local communities, and create opportunities to network with professionals and scientists who work in government, academia, or high-tech companies.

Suggested best practice.—To maximize these societal benefits, all USGS citizen-supported projects should:

- develop materials and processes to deliver age- and skill-appropriate training in their requisite technologies, protocols, and other techniques and share these resources through USGS, partner, and other citizen science-oriented knowledge portals; and

- for projects making explicit use of educational institutions' students and faculty, encourage and contribute to the design of formal study modules or curricula that incorporate project activities and findings.

Recruitment and Retention

Initially locating potential volunteers and keeping them engaged in long-term projects can be a daunting task. Many USGS project managers have voiced difficulty in their recruitment efforts to establish a robust volunteer base, or have encountered the situation where initial interest is high, but sustained involvement throughout the project duration is actually low. Below are some suggested techniques and methods from successful efforts.

Recruitment

Successful recruitment for projects requires:

- timely communication of opportunities, including clear descriptions of the overarching scientific questions being investigated, project goals and objectives, location and duration, time commitment and skills required, and other pertinent information; and

- personnel policies and processes be in place in the USGS that (a) can accommodate the variety of citizen-to-scientist relationships that characterize different types of projects and that (b) are easy to navigate and accomplish.

USGS science programs planning citizen-supported projects are encouraged to make use of existing communication channels and networks to identify and recruit suitable citizen science volunteers. These include:

- the USGS Office of Communications and Publishing, the USGS National Coordinator for Education, and the USGS Volunteer Program;

- existing Federal, State, agency, academic, and other partners; and

- community education, conservation, and similar civic groups in locales of interest.

Suggested best practice.—All opportunities for participation should be advertised through the Volunteer.gov portal.

Suggested best practice.—Science programs should consider creating and publishing public-oriented USGS Fact Sheets describing their citizen science-supported projects to cite or distribute as part of their recruiting efforts.

Suggested best practice.—The USGS should review and make any necessary revisions to the Volunteer for Science Handbook to assure that the recruitment process is as flexible and easy as possible.

Retention

Long-term retention of volunteers in whom we have invested time, energy, and resources to train, equip, and support should be a goal of every citizen science project. High turnover or loss of observers at critical junctures in a project can result in data loss or interruptions that may negatively impact its overall value or success.

The most effective means of assuring long-term interest and commitment to a project is to recognize, respect, communicate, and reward participants' contributions in ways that are meaningful to them. Successful citizen science initiatives reward participants in a variety of ways, including:

- sharing with them how their contributions have made a difference in answering a scientific question or in solving a problem by, for example, showing them resultant legislation;

- providing formal public or professional recognition of their contributions, including acknowledging them in formal scientific papers and reports or, if their level of contribution to project design or analysis warrants, sharing coauthorship;

- regularly communicating to them where progress is being made; and

- by showing them their individual data contributions in relation to the whole (for example, in a project database or analysis system) so that they know how their input is being used.

Ultimately, you must show them that you value their time, skills, and effort.

Other less sophisticated, but nevertheless useful, rewards and incentives may include personal thank you notes, small prizes, or newsletter articles focused on the individuals and their efforts. Online leaderboards or other competitions or challenges are also effective and fun ways to interact with volunteers and motivate them to stay involved in a program's activities.

Suggested best practice.—All USGS citizen science projects should identify, plan for, incorporate, and undertake or dispense appropriate participant incentives and rewards as a standard operating procedure.

Session Summary: Data Collection and Management

Introduction

Citizen Science projects utilize a number of methods and technologies to gather data from participants. For example, an individual project may support one or more of the following data-submission pathways: hand delivery, postal service mail, telephone calls, Web sites with data entry forms, email, text messaging, Twitter tweets, and custom-made mobile apps. Although the variety of data-collection methods is remarkably broad and a growing number of projects utilize modern technologies and social media to the fullest, that same variety also reveals a general lack of coordination. With so many possible means of gathering data, do they each provide the same level of data quality and reliability for each project? Which methods are the most appropriate for different kinds of projects?

Presently, each project is independent of the rest in terms of how the data are handled after they are acquired: where data are stored, the format and structure of the data, how they are quality assured, who has access to the data, and plans for long-term storage and sharing. Even if we consider only data taken using a single modality, there is a high likelihood that the data themselves are not handled in the same way by different research groups, and therefore, they may not be easily integrated when a blending of data is both reasonable and of scientific interest. Should we be creating data that are useful only for immediate project needs? What is needed to adjust our individualistic approaches towards the creation of an integrated set of observations?

One of the challenges ahead for citizen science is to capitalize on the wealth of experience and ingenuity that already exists for data capture and display, and to focus it into a set of uniform and robust methods and processes. These methods and processes can serve a variety of citizen science-supported research uses while ensuring data quality and fostering data standardization and interoperability. The "Data Collection and Management" session, facilitated by Steve Tessler, dealt with the overall importance of data management principles to the citizen science effort, the variety of data-capture techniques and their relevance to specific science goals, and the challenges of handling the data in a way that serves both researchers and the public.

Summary of Presentations

Andrea Wiggins described the efforts of the NSF-sponsored DataONE PPSR working group (PPSR is DataONE's term for citizen science—Public Participation in Scientific Research). The PPSR working group focuses on improving the quality, quantity, and accessibility of citizen-science data, and promoting the integration of those data into conventional science. DataONE's working groups are developing tools for creating data management plans (DMP), use cases, and management guides that help scientists see their role in data management activities.

A survey of scientists at a recent PPSR workshop indicated a general lack of data management planning; however, most prioritized four data support needs: analysis and visualization tools, data documentation, long-term storage, and consistent data policies (see PPSR workshop Evaluation Report).

Andrea Wiggins noted that the USGS can provide leadership in citizen science by sharing our formal data policies with the citizen science community and in developing and sharing broadly applicable technology platforms that others can use.

Austin Mast described the Integrated Digitized Biocollections (iDigBio) program, associated with the National Resource for Advancing Digitization of Biodiversity Collections. Only an estimated 10 percent of the 1 billion specimens in U.S. collections are currently digitized and accessible. An NSF program was developed to support the iDigBio goals, and several projects have been funded.

The goal of iDigBio is to create a permanent, digital database capable of housing all U.S. biological specimen collections, large and small. iDigBio will provide the technical infrastructure and expertise for storage, integration, search, and retrieval capabilities and of existing biological/paleontological specimen data, images, and other media files contributed by collaborating institutions into a cloud-based accessible interface using shared standards and formats.

The project provides opportunities to engage the public in activities, including specimen digitization (photography of 2- and 3-dimensional specimens and associated labeling), text transcription and specimen description, and georeferencing the specimens using a tool called GeoLocate. Recognition of volunteer effort is an important part of the program, including awarding service learning credits to student participants.

Hydrologist **Mike Fienen** discussed a low-cost citizen science effort that engages the public in monitoring water levels in streams. Mike has been involved with a groundwater monitoring network in Wisconsin where half of the observation stations are monitored by trained citizen volunteers. A chance introduction to the CrowdHydrology project from New York led him to craft a process and programming code to enable citizen observers to report stream levels by sending a text message indicating the site code and water level. Signage was kept to a minimum, indicating how to read the stream "height," a phone number to text the value and station code, and where to view their contribution online.

The messages are parsed using fuzzy logic and natural language processing techniques to identify the site code and stream height from the entire unstructured text message. Due to government policy issues, the values are stored in a delimited text file with a university. Because independent verification of reported values is not possible, data-quality management is focused on the processes that control data acquisition and parsing. The data can be viewed at a station Web site shortly after they are submitted by the contributors. Field validation using transducers, along with citizen reporting, indicated that the data are fairly good despite a few outliers.

The project is achieving its goal for involving citizens in real science, and found that locating a streamgage in areas where people regularly engage in nature study can increase participation. The code that supports the project is open source and available, and the method has been published and will be reused in an expanded project in the northeastern and north-central United States.

Tim Kern of the Fort Collins Science Center (FORT) described developments by the FORT support service software group of a multiagency framework for gathering public input data on the Web. This framework is reusable and can be extended to be used for other needs. From their experience, in order to effectively work within policy guidelines when collecting information from the public, researchers should:

- limit data collection to the minimum detail needed,

- encrypt personal information collected and stored,

- use agency-approved technologies,

- define data-integrity requirements,

- develop metadata in process,

- have data reviewed by a data steward prior to public release, and

- create early connections from the data to USGS publications.

Tim Kern's group recommends that agencies and the public interact with the data via Web services connected to a secure geodatabase housed at an enterprise repository (for example, at the USGS, or other trusted institution, rather than with a free service or startup site on the Web). One example of an enterprise repository available at the USGS is the ScienceBase system. ScienceBase serves individuals and teams with tools for uploading and managing data and metadata, and provides various end-use tools to access the information.

Derek Masaki demonstrated a simple observation application that collects data using email, Twitter, or text message. Parsing the meaning of the data from multiple input formats is relatively easy only when the data requested are simple. Government IT priorities are moving towards providing open data any time on any device, creating APIs, and using social media methods to both collect data and produce data awareness among the citizenry.

Misconceptions about citizen science data are that the information gathered is inferior, and that online information cannot be trusted. Creating "open-data" resources allows review and improvement of data to be done by the crowd, and can lead to new uses and better validated data. Rather than creating enterprise software for users, agencies can devote that effort to creating a quality-data resource and pushing the data to the crowd to empower them—and let them develop the tools they need.

Schools, in particular, represent an untapped pool of potential observers who can provide a wealth of data from across the Nation. Students can benefit from learning about science in the context of their own communities. By developing volunteer networks at the county level and providing training for various observation types, we could leverage citizen-data-collection efforts to build nationally consistent datasets. The future vision is to develop a national biological monitoring network of volunteers to conduct a biodiversity survey, where our role is to provide a mobile standard for reporting scientific observations as an open-data resource based on a common service API.

Facilitated Discussion Highlights

The following topics were discussed after the presentations:

- Documentation: Documentation of data and processes in a citizen science workflow is highly variable. Some but not all projects publish the details of their collection strategy and programming; in fact, it is becoming more common for teams to work in open-source environments to encourage interaction with the broader community of developers. Data management plans are not common and tools are being developed for USGS researchers; however, in general, each dataset should be accompanied by a project metadata record with a data dictionary, and each file and record needs a unique identifier to help manage the provenance of data. USGS data are often tagged either as provisional or approved, but a third classification is needed for citizen science data that are not fully vetted and cannot be checked at the source.

- Quality Control: Quality control in citizen science projects is done mostly at the point of data acquisition. Location attributes are widely known for their dubious quality issues, and it is a good practice to provide some redundancy, such as coordinate values accompanied by State and county. Even consulting cell-provider coverage maps can be important when considering where to position data-collection stations. The Great Sunflower Project (a national bee survey) uses multiple means of curating location data. Discover Life protocols include photographing a clock to show correct time and a GPS for location coordinates.

- Images: Images were actively discussed as a valuable component of many citizen science projects. DataONE found that a third of projects surveyed included images as part of their data collection. Modern image files have a data segment that stores metadata such as title, author, date and time, camera settings, location, copyright, and other attributes. We should be taking more advantage of those file properties when collecting image data, and consider them when developing protocols and training, such as checking the camera date and time before making observations. Some cameras have built-in GPS for capturing coordinates, and there are other methods to add them later using GPS tracks or mapping software. The colors in images are affected by the type of illumination; photography using a natural-light balanced flash device will be more accurate when there is a need to capture true and consistent color.

- Data Preservation: Regarding data preservation, large national projects, such as the USGS National Water Information System (NWIS) and the USGS National Water-Quality Assessment Program (NAWQA), can support their data with staff and infrastructure, but there is no corporate strategy for long-term storage of all data. There are a growing number of options for outside data storage (see the Directory of Open Access Repositories), but there is concern under Federal records policy about whether it is appropriate for data for USGS projects to be deposited in outside repositories. There was a consensus that the USGS should build a repository for data that do not have a corporate home. Although data sharing can be viewed as one method for preserving data, issues of synchronization and duplication due to data sharing between repositories need to be considered. Use of commercial social media sites, such as Facebook and Flickr, are inappropriate for storage because there is no long-term commitment or guarantee and TOS change frequently.

- Image Storage: There are many options available for projects to store image files. MorphBank is an open code project to assist developers with establishing an image library for a project. Discover Life stores and processes images and has an agreement with DOI for long-term curation. Cloud storage is also available for citizen science uses (for example,

Google's Picassa and Flickr). The Bird Phenology Program handles scanned images of paper records, not specimens, and ancillary information can be associated with the images.

- Data Formats: All in attendance agreed that Web services and APIs are important for delivering data; however, most data customers do not access data via those routes and prefer getting prepackaged data in a format they can use. That may mean serving data as spreadsheets, delimited text files, a geodatabase, or any other currently acceptable data-file format in addition to XML. Spreadsheets remain popular with research users regardless of how data professionals view the format and software. Researchers can collect and store data in a variety of formats. Perceived standards can sometimes be an impediment to data storage and sharing because formats change over time. More than one recommendation was to use delimited text files for data storage and exchange, and to develop translators to read user formats and produce output for users.

Observations and Suggested Best Practices

Approaches to Data Management

Data management planning can be a valuable aid in preparing for and carrying out citizen science-supported research projects. Addressing the full data management life cycle in citizen science projects is important for creating quality data that properly acknowledge the effort of volunteer participants and preserves the data for future use. The only differentiation between "regular" data and citizen science data are that these data are collected by volunteers. If all the steps and processes for how the data are collected and handled are documented, ensuring its fitness for reuse, one should be confident in what the data mean and how they can be used. This is true of any data, not just volunteer-collected data.

There are three typical approaches to data management in citizen science programs: (1) simple data entry forms on a Web site or on paper; (2) a deployed content management system; or (3) a customized digital platform. There are three main kinds of customized platforms that exist: (1) observation based; (2) transcription based; and (3) image based.

Suggested best practice.—The USGS should adopt existing open-source solutions and share them broadly instead of recreating solutions that already exist. Collectively, we will make greater strides on the science when we are not bogged down with technological hurdles.

Suggested best practice.—Perceptions of poor data quality due to utilizing volunteers and volunteer-collected data can be easily dismissed if you document data-collection protocols, reuse existing adopted standards, require images with species reports, and demonstrate repeatability of methods.

Suggested best practice.—The USGS needs to establish some basic guidelines for providing unique identifiers for data; data provenance tracking; data documentation; and handling of image, sound, and video files used in research projects. The USGS also needs to develop a national repository for data that have no corporate home, and guarantee the curation of those data as an asset for the long term.

Active and Passive Data Collection

Data collection with cell phones and smartphones is inevitable. In the United States, 80 percent of adults have cell phones and 40 percent have smartphones, although these figures are heavily biased toward those living in coastal or urban areas. Several open-source, natural language-processing tools have been developed to translate text messages into useful data. Currently, this software is being used for hydrological and earthquake data, but it could be adapted to interpret any observation or measurement. At this time, crowdHydrology software can be downloaded and used by anyone, and tweets are being interpreted for the early detection of earthquakes in the TED program.

Social media and crowdsourcing can provide data needed to rapidly detect and broadcast events in hazardous or emergency situations. With the proper infrastructure in place to receive the data, these signals can provide faster notification of events than compiling data from sensors on the ground.

Standards Versus Data Translation

Suggested best practice.—Citizen science projects should establish the minimum data needed from citizen science participants as a good strategy to minimize issues with data policies, acquisition modalities, data-processing complexity, quality control, storage, and sharing.

Individual file structures and handling will continue to be an issue, so deciding on data exchange formats rather than supporting multiple data translations is economical. Translators can be built to convert common data to user-requested formats for sharing.

Characteristics of Government-Funded Projects

A survey conducted during a PPSR workshop in August 2012 found that government-funded projects (for example, NSF):

- were least satisfied with their current processes for sharing data with colleagues, and the ways in which they could present the data to their volunteer participants;

- were further ahead in documenting or having data management plans and practices in place than about half of the broader community, who said they had no data management plan nor were they in the process of developing one;

- strongly desired assistance with analyzing and visualizing data, documenting and describing data, and voiced a need for training in data management practices.

Suggested best practice.—The USGS can have a positive impact on the broader citizen science community by being an active participant; leading the way on data sharing and publishing; making our data policies available and easy to find; sharing with everyone our technology developments; describing our data-quality methods clearly; and lending credibility to citizen science activities by our very involvement.

Development Considerations

Potential developers of mobile apps need to be aware that native apps provide a means for local storage while Web-based HTML5 mobile apps require a network connection. There are also hybrid apps being developed that may provide the best of both options.

FORT has a long history of developing software and infrastructure, including tools that apply to engaging the public in monitoring and communication about needs on Federal lands. These tools also provide back-end data management and infrastructure to the employees and staff who need to access and archive this information. Developers can consult FORT or others for development best practices and methods.

Common Observation Standard

Suggested best practice.—Observational information, including the core set of information needed for environmental studies (what is being observed, where, when, and by whom?), should be as natural and familiar to everyone as addressing an envelope. Scientists should drive this observation standard among all citizen science projects.

Strategies in Information Technology

There are several information technology strategies that are driving government priorities for citizen science initiatives:
- Provide open data as a default.

- Make information and data available anytime on any device.

- Provide access to data and information as an API—meaning portable and usable in other systems in standard ways.

- Do not force people into programs or solutions you envision for them.

- Make government data social.

- Change the meaning of social participation by leveraging the community in ways that show practical value.

Suggested best practice.—In designing citizen science applications, we should remember that society already views opinions as valuable in many social situations (applications like Yelp!, Amazon reviews, Facebook "likes," and reviews of restaurants or movies). We should consider leveraging this type of evaluation system for use in science.

The open publication of data will lead to new discoveries and improve the value and need for the data. The USGS needs to focus on making our data available for other uses and enlisting more users; for example, through Data.gov (*http://www.data.gov/*). Experience points to the need to offer both preformatted file types, such as xml, shp, mdb, xls, ppt, jpg, or Google documents, and even simpler formats, such as txt or csv. All data should also be accompanied by adequate metadata to identify its source and quality constraints. A few groups make use of available APIs and are tech savvy enough to do so, but most are not very familiar with them or do not know how to apply them. The reality is that large amounts of data are still collected in Excel and (or) Access. The USGS Center for Integrated Data Analytics (CIDA) takes an intermediate approach to this by creating Web tools to interact with data in a variety of formats. For work on integration projects, it is best to avoid forcing standards adoption and to work on translating between a central, agreed-upon standard and that of the data provider.

Suggested best practice.—The USGS should consider what activities will require human intervention to make or confirm an observation or create and improve data, and what can be done without the use of volunteers by natural language processing, machine learning, or calculation by algorithms. We must be respectful of our volunteers' time.

Session Summary: Technology and Tools

Introduction

The technology and tools session, chaired by Derek Masaki, provided an overview of existing tools and infrastructure available for use in support of citizen science projects. Citizen science efforts are often run with limited budgets, and often have much to gain by leveraging existing technology, protocols, and standards. Most of the applications presented are open and available for any group to adopt and customize to suit specific needs. Jennifer Hammock, John Pickering, and Isla Young presented external experiences and approaches for information capture, data management, and infrastructure needs in support of citizen science programs, while Derek Masaki and Jessica Zelt shared examples of current USGS solutions for supporting crowdsourcing activities and mobile device observation collection.

Summary of Presentations

Jennifer Hammock highlighted the features and capabilities provided by the EOL platform. She demonstrated a number of tools that are available to support and benefit citizen science efforts, particularly volunteer species observation events such as regional BioBlitzes. Jennifer also provided many examples of projects that are using EOL for data upload, the vetting of information, and as a point of dissemination that demonstrates its flexibility.

EOL also:

- Creates customized field guides, lowering the barrier to entry for production of Web-available material with rich content. Small groups or K–12 classrooms could take advantage of the service to design species guides for very small areas (such as a backyard, a school ground, or a regional park).

- Provides APIs that can be utilized by external entities interested in querying available species data. The API responds in JSON and XML formats.

- Automates additions to EOL's photo archive by autoharvesting volunteer species image contributions from Flickr images and their tags from a specific EOL group.

- Draws from the EOL community to assist with species identification.

- Connects with content partners such as SoundCloud, Vimeo and Youtube, providing multiple conduits for information flow to EOL.

For those interested in becoming a content partner, there are instructions at *http://eol.org/info/cp_getting_started*.

Derek Masaki shared experiences from the August 2012 DC/Baltimore Cricket Crawl, an extension of the 2009 New York Cricket Crawl event. This event involved citizen scientists, artists, naturalists, and casual participants for an evening sound census of the late summer crickets and katydids singing throughout the Baltimore/DC metro areas. Derek Masaki led a discussion on the methods used in the survey, provided a short overview of outcomes, and provided guidance on conducting your own local neighborhood cricket survey.

The DC/Baltimore Cricket Crawl drew in over 300 participants, surveyed more than 400 sites, and generated approximately 2,000 cricket and katydid observations submitted via Twitter, SMS Text, phone calls, and email, with over 75 percent of reports shared through email.

The event proved that low-cost, lightweight, mobile-based platforms can bring in hundreds of volunteers, participating in events that generate thousands of new species observations, many in areas that have not been previously surveyed.

Jessica Zelt presented her experiences with the USGS Bird Phenology Program, which collected six million paper records of patterns of bird migration between 1881 and 1970. For 40 years, the cards were filed into offsite file cabinets, before climate change research provided the impetus for resurrecting and digitizing the information contained on the stored cards.

The project relies upon crowdsourcing the digitization of the cards to its network of over 2,500 volunteers. Cards containing species, location, observer, and date of arrival are converted to digital text using a Web application that facilitates transcription of scanned information into a database format. Statistics that track transcription progress are made public and the volunteer effort has turned into a competitive endeavor, with a few of the top contributors digitizing over 150,000 records. Of the one million scanned records, 600,000 have been digitally transcribed by the network of volunteers.

John Pickering presented an overview of the Discover Life program and its functions to support citizen science initiatives, as well as a summary of the volunteer-driven Mothing project. As an active participant, John wakes up at 4:00 a. m. each morning to conduct observation sessions, which include photographing and counting moths attracted to porch lights near his home.

Discover Life's methods and monitoring protocols allow for the rapid collection, sharing, and integration of vast quantities of high-quality data from numerous study sites using digital photography and an easy-to-use suite of online tools for uploading and organizing images. The protocol includes steps such as photographing GPS devices and cell phones, which provides project administrators confidence in verifying the reported location and time-stamp information for the monitoring event.

Discover Life also provides species identification assistance, as well as the ability to produce self-validating, location-based guides based on previous reports.

Discover Life provides an outstanding model and working system that the emerging USGS citizen science effort can utilize in developing a national, volunteer-driven observation network for the aggregation, dissemination, and analysis of information pertaining to natural resource conservation.

Isla Young manages and is involved in several programs in Hawaii with a mission to develop science and technology talent by introducing K–12 students to STEM fields through hands-on learning and focused workshops. Students passing through these programs are also eligible for academic and professional placements (through scholarships and internship opportunities).

Students have opportunities to learn and use technology in collaboration with local businesses and researchers to solve real local problems, including GIS, Computer Aided Design (CAD), programming, robotics, and cyber security, for example. The programs are constantly evolving to incorporate emerging trends. Participants are reminded that they have a responsibility to serve as role models and leaders after they complete their academic journey and enter the workforce. There is a strong emphasis on community and citizenship.

Isla encouraged the USGS Citizen Science Working Group to advance outreach efforts to the K–12 education community. Initiatives that build bridges between science agencies and education are an opportunity to benefit all participants. Students could serve as a volunteer observation corps for the USGS—armed with mobile technology—and could easily add thousands of new observations applicable to science investigations of water quality, ecosystem health, or air quality.

Facilitated Discussion Highlights

The following topics were discussed after the presentations:

- Data Review Status: Depending on the partner and their observation sources, EOL assigns a status for how imported data appear in their system with project manager input. If the partner decides that there are appropriate review procedures completed before import, they are marked as reviewed or trusted on the site. Those data that are imported from sources, such as Flickr, which may require additional scrutiny and attention, are marked as unreviewed and can be easily found by curators to change the status after curation procedures are completed.

- Geolocation of Audio Files: Currently, if audio files are shared with EOL, geolocation information is stored in plain text, and does not generate point layers of data as a regular practice. EOL can work with partners to generate specific displays of geographic information, but it is recommended to use a repository specifically aimed at housing this information, such as the Global Biodiversity Information Facility or the Macaulay Library.

- Reusable Architecture: The Bird Phenology Program architecture and network established may continue beyond its initial purpose to take advantage of the existing volunteers organized for other tasks, such as reporting first date arrivals for migratory birds or to digitize bird stomach contents cards similar to the migratory bird card project. Because digital or computerized distinction of overlapping animal calls is limited, there were suggestions from the audience and discussion on reuse of the system to potentially crowdsource sound-recording identification using volunteers.

- Technological Advancement: As technology improves and is more broadly accessible, less-specialized equipment and software may be necessary to capture audio from animals and insects. Where once it was required to have specific programs and extra microphone attachments to capture higher frequency sounds and more variable audio ranges, smartphones are now able to capture audio, upload files, and allow users to manage observations and link audio files in a simple manner.

- Volunteer Efforts: If a machine can easily do the work, have a machine do the work. Use volunteers instead to perform tasks that computers do poorly (for example, discerning between overlapping audio calls). When assigning species or objects to volunteers for observation, stick to those that are easily distinguished by volunteers in their area, versus those that require spore prints, DNA samples, or expert knowledge to successfully identify.

- Crossing Communities: There are many opportunities (other than biological observation collection) for engaging different communities with regard to citizen and partner participation. Collaborations could be developed with computer scientists, where tasks may be developing infrastructure or applications to gamify science (including mechanics of games, such as levels, badges, and rewards). Partnerships with statisticians could be developed for analyzing real science data from your community. Beyond science and math, those proficient in marketing and sales may help get involved to hone outreach and engagement approaches.

Observations and Suggested Best Practices

Adopting Existing Infrastructure

Existing platforms can provide some stability to new initiatives, since there may be little-to-no cost for using the existing infrastructure, and the new program can focus funds on other needs, like outreach and training efforts, for their volunteers. Volunteers may be already familiar with using online services like Flickr, YouTube, SoundCloud, and Vimeo, so consider these existing systems for managing media files or other functional needs.

Suggested best practice.—The USGS should look at reusing or incorporating its own infrastructure (or partner systems that the agency may have helped develop) and extend the reach and accessibility of its development efforts. Volunteers may be interested in expanding their activities if they are already familiar with the technology being used.

The technologies discussed do more than just allow the involvement of citizens as sensors for observations or other measurements. They also provide the infrastructure to crowdsource imagery or other onscreen records into digital records, or to capture more detailed information for analytical purposes.

Crowdsourcing Development of Infrastructure

To support citizen science infrastructure development and research needs, Sally Holl, from the USGS Texas Water Science Center, suggested reviewing a proposal she wrote in early 2012 (Code for Science: Unleashing the Power of Volunteers and Open Data to Improve Earth Science) that calls for organizing a crowdsourced competition, spurring innovation and creative developments with USGS data in support of its research.

Several others at the workshop are interested in an upcoming opportunity to be posted to Challenge.gov through the Core Systems Analytics and Synthesis (CSAS) group at USGS (*http://applifyingusgsdata.challenge.gov/*). The challenge, titled "Applifying USGS Earth Science Data," is looking for developers and data visualization specialists to create new applications utilizing CSAS datasets. Since this is the first challenge put forth by the USGS, it will serve as a precedent for future postings. CSS leadership is supportive and available to push efforts ahead if we encounter hurdles moving forward.

Postworkshop Actions

From the presentation contents, discussions, and suggestions shared throughout the workshop, the CSWG and USGS would benefit the community of researchers at the workshop by supporting efforts to:

- Develop a decision tree for researchers and scientists to navigate applicable policies and provide digestible details on how project design decisions may affect the approach to policy.

- Identify a subgroup to consider justifications for a separation or distinction between citizen science engagement and existing volunteer activities and suggest solutions to fill gaps in policy or guidance.

- Create a subgroup to identify and educate others about USGS' citizen science activities, highlighting successes, especially aimed towards leadership audiences and those who can positively affect current roadblocks and challenges to success.

- Look for opportunities across CDI and the USGS to collaborate on citizen science aspects within other areas of active research (for example, data management life cycle, mobile-application development, usability and human-computer interactions, and visualizations).

- Decide on a strategy for formalizing USGS/CSWG engagement with other citizen-science research communities and working groups. Share outputs that these communities can benefit from, such as data policies and infrastructure solutions.

- Raise awareness of existing work available that can be leveraged by scientists to kick-start projects and save them resources and time.

- Identify opportunities for connecting USGS science with informal education programs, with educators and STEM programs, and with other communities.

- Create a group to research, develop, and adopt a common observation standard to facilitate data integration across citizen science efforts.

- Support creation of a formal Web site to serve: (1) as a platform to facilitate communication and collaboration with internal and external researchers, partners, and volunteers; and (2) as a knowledge resource to collect, organize, and share tools, techniques, protocols, and other information relevant to the design and execution of citizen-supported USGS science projects.

- Promote, celebrate, and get the word out about USGS citizen science opportunities and successes over the Web, at professional meetings and community events, and through publications.

References Cited

Bonney, Rick, Ballard, Heidi, Jordan, Rebecca, McCallie, Ellen, Phillips, Tina, Shirk, Jennifer, and Wilderman, C.C. 2009, Public participation in scientific research; Defining the field and assessing its potential for informal science education: Washington, D.C., Center for Advancement of Informal Science Education (CAISE), 58 p., at *http://caise.insci.org/uploads/docs/ PPSR%20report%20FINAL.pdf.*

Catlin-Groves, C.L., 2012, The citizen science landscape; From volunteers to citizen sensors and beyond: International Journal of Zoology, v. 2012, Article ID 349630, 14 p. (Also available at *http://dx.doi.org/10.1155/2012/349630.*)

Dickinson, J.L., Zuckerberg, Benjamin, and Bonter, D.N., 2010, Citizen science as an ecological research tool; Challenges and benefits: Annual Review of Ecology, Evolution, and Systematics, v. 41, p. 149–172. (Also available at *http://dx.doi. org/10.1146/annurev-ecolsys-102209-144636.*)

Droege, Sam, 2007, Just because you paid them doesn't mean their data are better: Citizen Science Toolkit Conference, Cornell Lab of Ornithology, Ithaca, New York, June 20–23, 2007, 14 p., accessed June 7, 2013, at *http://www.birds.cornell.edu/ citscitoolkit/features/resolveuid/ec5b58393f28553698cb6501959e26d4.*

Duke, Monica, 2012, Citizen science: DCC Briefing Papers, Digital Curation Centre, Edinburgh, accessed June 7, 2013, at *http://www.dcc.ac.uk/resources/briefing-papers/citizen science*.

Haklay, Muki, 2010, How good is volunteered geographical information? A comparative study of OpenStreetMap and Ordnance Survey datasets: Environment and Planning B; Planning and Design, v. 37, no. 4, p. 682–703. (Also available at *http://dx.doi.org/10.1068/b35097*.)

Lee, Tracey, Quinn, M.S., and Duke, Danah, 2006, Citizen, science, highways, and wildlife; Using a Web-based GIS to engage citizens in collecting wildlife information: Ecology and Society, v. 11, no. 1, article 11, accessed June 7, 2013, at *http://www.ecologyandsociety.org/vol11/iss1/art11/*.

Miller-Rushing, Abraham, Primack, Richard, and Bonney, Rick, 2012, The history of public participation in ecological research: Frontiers in Ecology and the Environment, v. 10, no. 6, p. 285–290. (Also available at *http://dx.doi.org/10.1890/110278*.)

Nielsen, Michael, 2011, Reinventing discovery; The new era of networked science: Princeton, Princeton University Press, 272 p.

Schwartz, M.D., Betancourt, J.L., and Weltzin, J.F., 2012, From Caprio's lilacs to the U.S.A. National Phenology Network: Frontiers in Ecology and the Environment, v. 10, no. 6, p. 324–327. (Also available at *http://dx.doi.org/10.1890/110281*.)

Shirk, J.L., Ballard, H.L., Wilderman, C.C., Phillips, Tina, Wiggins, Andrea, Jordan, Rebecca, McCallie, Ellen, Minarchek, Matthew, Lewenstein, B.V., Krasny, M.E., and Bonney, Rick, 2012, Public participation in scientific research; A framework for deliberate design: Ecology and Society, v. 17, no. 2, article 29. (Also available at *http://dx.doi.org/10.5751/ES-04705-170229*.)

Silvertown, Jonathan, 2009, A new dawn for citizen science: Trends in Ecology & Evolution, v. 24, no. 9, p. 467–471. (Also available at *http:/dx.doi.org/10.1016/j.tree.2009.03.017*.)

Trumbull, D.J., Bonney, Rick, Bascom, Derek, and Cabral, Anna, 2000, Thinking scientifically during participation in a citizen science project: Science Education, v. 84, issue 2, p. 265–275.

U.S. Geological Survey, 2007, Facing tomorrow's challenges—U.S. Geological Survey science in the decade 2007–2017: U.S. Geological Survey Circular 1309, 69 p. (Also available at *http://pubs.usgs.gov/circ/2007/1309/*.)

Wald, D.J, Quitoriano, Vincent, Worden, C.B., Hopper, Margaret, and Dewey, J.W., 2011, USGS "Did You Feel It?" Internet-based macroseismic intensity maps: Annals of Geophysics, v. 54, no. 6, p. 688–707. (Also available at *http:/dx.doi.org/10.4401/ag-5354*.)

Weltzin, J.F., 2011, The USA National Phenology Network; Taking the pulse of our planet: U.S. Geological Survey Fact Sheet 2011–3023, 4 p. (Also available at *http://pubs.usgs.gov/fs/2011/3023/*.)

Appendix A.   Participants

Name	Title	Organization	Location	Email
Shari Baloch	Program Analyst	USGS	Reston, VA	smbaloch@usgs.gov
Abigail Benson	Biologist	USGS	Denver, CO	albenson@usgs.gov
Beau Bouchard	Geographer	USGS	Golden, CO	beau@beaubouchard.com
Sky Bristol	Manager	USGS	Denver, CO	sbristol@usgs.gov
Matthew Cannister	Biological Technician	USGS	Gainesville, FL	mcannister@usgs.gov
Jennifer Chipault	Biological Technician	USGS	Madison, WI	jchipault@usgs.gov
Joshua Dein	Veterinary Medical Officer	USGS	Madison, WI	fjdein@usgs.gov
Meg Domroese	Conservation Project Leader		Madison, WI	megdom1@gmail.com
Paul Earle	Geophysicist	USGS	Denver, CO	pearle@usgs.gov
Elisabeth Faulk	Volunteer	USGS	Denver, CO	liz faulk@gmail.com
Michael Fienen	Research Hydrologist, Groundwater Specialist	USGS	Middleton, WI	mnfienen@usgs.gov
Kevin Gallagher	Associate Director Core Science Systems	USGS	Reston, VA	kgallagher@usgs.gov
Diane Garcia	Cartographer	USGS	Menlo Park, CA	dgarcia@usgs.gov
David Govoni	Physical Scientist	USGS	Reston, VA	dgovoni@usgs.gov
Linda Gundersen	Director, Office of Science Quality and Integrity	USGS	Reston, VA	lgundersen@usgs.gov
Muki Haklay	Professor	University College London	London, UK	m haklay@ucl.ac.uk
Jen Hammock	Encyclopedia of Life Marine Theme Coordinator	Smithsonian Institution	Washington, D.C.	hammock@si.edu
Emily Himmelstoss	Geologist	USGS	Woods Hole, MA	ehimmelstoss@usgs.gov
Megan Hines	Technical Manager	University of Wisconsin	Madison, WI	mkhines@wisc.edu
Sally Holl	Geographer	USGS	Austin, TX	sholl@usgs.gov
Barb Horn	Water Resource Specialist	State of Colorado	Durango, CO	barb horn@state.co.us
Tim Kern	Computer Engineer	USGS	Fort Collins, CO	kernt@usgs.gov
Erin Korris	Geographer	USGS	Denver, CO	ekorris@usgs.gov
Sophia Liu	Research Geographer	USGS	Denver, CO	sophialiu@usgs.gov
Derek Masaki	Biological Data Manager/ Geospatial Liaison	USGS	Reston, VA	dmasaki@usgs.gov
Austin Mast	Associate Professor	Florida State University	Tallahassee, FL	amast@bio.fsu.edu
Greg Matthews	Project Manager	USGS	Denver, CO	gdmatthews@usgs.gov

Cheryl Morris	Director, Core Science Analytics and Synthesis	USGS	Denver, CO	cmorris@usgs.gov
David Newman	FOIA/Privacy Officer	USGS	Reston, VA	djnewman@usgs.gov
Greg Newman	Ecologist/Web Designer	Colorado State University	Fort Collins, CO	gregory_newman@colostate.edu
John Pickering	Discover Life Project Leader	Polistes Foundation / University of Georgia	Athens, GA	pick@discoverlife.org
Barbara Poore	Geographer	USGS	St. Petersburg, FL	bspoore@usgs.gov
Lorna Schmid	Infrastructure and Operations Team Lead	USGS	Reston, VA	lorna@usgs.gov
Linda Schueck	Information Technology Specialist	USGS	Boise, ID	lschueck@usgs.gov
Jennifer Shirk	CitizenScience.org Project Leader	Cornell University	Ithaca, NY	jls223@cornell.edu
Laura Smyrl	Technology Specialist/ Project Manager	USGS	Fort Collins, CO	lsmyrl@usgs.gov
Annie Simpson	Biologist and Information Scientist	USGS	Reston, VA	asimpson@usgs.gov
Cheryl Smith	Human Capital Management Officer	USGS	Reston, VA	cherylsm@usgs.gov
Michael Speak	Supervisory Cartographer	USGS	Rolla, MO	mspeak@usgs.gov
Cathy Tate	Ecologist	USGS	Denver, CO	cmtate@usgs.gov
Steven Tessler	Ecologist/Data Manager	USGS	W. Trenton, NJ	stessler@usgs.gov
Robert Thieler	Research Geologist	USGS	Woods Hole, MA	rthieler@usgs.gov
Randy Updike	Regional Executive Rocky Mountain Area	USGS	Denver, CO	updike@usgs.gov
Kristi Wallace	Geologist	USGS	Anchorage, AK	kwallace@usgs.gov
Ben Wheeler	Biological Information Specialist	USGS	Denver, CO	bwheeler@usgs.gov
Andrea Wiggins	Postdoctoral Fellow	Cornell University	Ithaca, NY	andrea.wiggins@cornell.edu
Eric Wolf	Geographer	USGS	Denver, CO	ebwolf@usgs.gov
Isla Young	Director K12 STEM Education, Women in Technology	Maui Economic Development Board	Maui, HI	isla@medb.org
Jessica Zelt	Program Coordinator	USGS	Laurel, MD	jzelt@usgs.gov

Appendix B.   Plenary Session Abstracts

If available, presentations are linked from their title to a copy stored for retrieval. Authors whose abstract titles are not linked should be contacted directly for access. Supplemental Web links are included where they have been supplied by the authors.

Exploring the Landscape of Citizen Science and Public Participation in Scientific Research

Jennifer Shirk, Project Leader, Cornell Lab of Ornithology

http://www.citizenscience.org
http://www.citizenscience.org/community/conference2012/post-conference/

Given the large (and growing) landscape of citizen science, how might invested individuals and organizations work together to collectively map out and navigate the diverse and sometimes rocky terrain? We will explore a corner of this land-scape together, looking for:

- the opportunities that citizen science offers for science, education, and societal outcomes;

- what we can learn from the choices made by researchers in other citizen science initiatives; and

- how we (as individuals, and as representatives of an organization such as the USGS) can be part of advancing a field of practice for PPSR.

Ensuring Legal and Policy Compliant Citizen Science App Development

Lorna Schmid, Infrastructure and Operations Team Lead, USGS Administration and Enterprise Information

The CDI-sponsored USGS Mobile Framework poster reflects the components required to ensure a well-supported community that promotes the development and use of mobile technologies to further science. The initial focus of the project included creation of draft workflows meant to facilitate and expedite, and to provide quality assurance of mobile application development and deployment across the USGS. The longer term project recommendations include: institution of a recognized mobile community of practice to support development and use of the Mobile Framework; reviewing and communicating policy requirements, guidelines, and procedures to the community; and the establishment of a formal process for managing and supporting USGS mobile applications as products. Additionally, a one-stop shop to support the inherent hardware/device management, application development, application delivery, and life-cycle management components encompassed by this framework will be developed.

iPlover: A Smartphone Application to Characterize Piping Plover Nest Locations

Robert Thieler, Research Geologist, USGS Woods Hole Coastal and Marine Science Center

http://wh.er.usgs.gov/slr/

iPlover is a mobile device application intended to collect location and environmental attribute information for Piping Plover (Charadrius melodus) nests. iPlover uses HTML5 and JavaScript to provide a simple data form that can be filled out rapidly and efficiently in the field. The data are transmitted over the Internet to a central database, where they are quality checked, archived, and subsequently used as input into research models of plover habitat evolution and utilization.

Atlantic coast Piping Plovers are a threatened species for which there are active management efforts at annual and longer time scales. iPlover users are trained plover monitors. They are a diverse group, representing Federal and State agencies, non-governmental organizations, land-owning trusts, and private citizen volunteers. The monitors have a wide variety of expertise (or lack thereof) in environmental assessment. iPlover provides a common tool and protocols that standardize data collection and quality control, and thus it facilitates research.

Preliminary work indicates that key parameters needed to predict nest locations, density, and outcome (for example, modes of nest failure, or hatching and fledging of chicks) can be collected quickly and efficiently. The collected data enhances ongoing work by the USGS, Fish and Wildlife Service, and collaborators to create robust models of plover habitat evolution and nest-site selection under alternative forecasts of rising sea level and changing storminess throughout the plover breeding range from North Carolina to Nova Scotia. iPlover is a specific example of a generalizable approach to distributed monitoring of physical and ecological systems that supports research, management, education, and outreach that can enable better stewardship of the coastal environment.

USGS Volunteer Program and Handbook

Cheryl Smith, Program Analyst, USGS Volunteer Program

http://internal.usgs.gov/ops/hro/recruit/volunteerhandbook.pdf

The presentation is a brief overview of the official USGS Volunteer for Science Program. The Volunteer Program is comprised of a diverse group of individuals who contribute to the USGS mission in many ways. Retired scientists and technical experts often continue to participate in USGS activities as Scientist Emeriti under the Volunteer Program. These volunteer positions enable Scientist Emeriti to complete their research, write up the results, and provide expertise and counsel in support of USGS projects and programs. Other volunteers contribute to the USGS by performing duties in the field, in laboratories, or in support functions. An individual who volunteers under the USGS Volunteer for Science Program must sign an agreement with a project manager or supervisor to perform specific duties within a specified period of time. The agreement (Volunteer Services Agreement for Natural Resources Agencies/OF-301A) is used by the bureaus under the DOI. The USGS recognizes the valuable contributions of volunteers and participates in a workgroup comprised of members of the DOI bureaus and other agencies to promote volunteer opportunities for individuals.

How Are USGS Citizen Projects Impacted by Government Policies?

Eric Wolf, Geographer, USGS Center of Excellence in GIS, and Barbara Poore, Geographer, USGS St. Petersburg Coastal and Marine Science Center

Citizen science projects are currently covered by several Federal and USGS-specific policies that govern the interactions of Federal agencies with the public. These include the Privacy Act of 1974, the PRA of 1995, and the USGS Volunteer for Science Handbook. These regulations do not account for the different ways in which citizen science projects are practiced in the age of the Internet and mobile technologies. None of these documents take into account the Open Government Directive of 2009 and the White House Memorandum on the use of Social Media of 2010, which would seem to give permission for an expanded range of activities with respect to how scientists can engage the public.

For example, the Volunteer Handbook addresses liability issues that arise from volunteers handling firearms and rafting the Colorado, but imagines that citizen science activities always involve personal contact between the scientist and the citizen. Many citizen science activities take place entirely online, with citizens contributing data or identifying photographs. There is no way to fingerprint those who work more than 180 days, as suggested in the handbook. In addition, these regulations do not deal with people from other countries who might contribute to an online mapping application, the vast possibilities for mobile data collection, or the privacy implications of gathering data from Twitter users who do not know that their data is being "mined." We suggest a review of these documents in light of present practices and future trajectories of citizen science projects at the USGS.

Three Laws Impacting Science Activities

Shari Baloch, Program Analyst, USGS Administration and Enterprise Information; and David Newman, FOIA/Privacy Officer, USGS Administration and Enterprise Information
http://pubs.usgs.gov/gip/140/GIP140.pdf

Congress enacted the PRA of 1995 to minimize the burden that the Government imposes on the public and to improve the quality and use of Federal information. The Act requires Federal agencies to establish an independent review process for information collection. Federal agencies must seek and obtain OMB approval before undertaking a collection of information directed to 10 or more persons.

Examples of information collection include (but are not limited to):

- grant application forms,

- written forms or surveys,

- permit application forms,

- telephone surveys, and

- electronic data collection.

The FOIA, 5 U.S.C. § 552, as amended, generally provides that any person has a right to request access to Federal agency records. The USGS proactively promotes information disclosure as inherent to its mission of providing objective science to inform decisionmakers and the general public. USGS scientists disseminate up-to-date and historical scientific data that are critical to addressing national and global priorities.

The PRA of 1974 5 U.S.C. § 552(a), requires that Federal employees and contractors protect PII, such as Social Security number, cell phone number, email address, private residence address, or other information that can be traced back to an individual. Prior to approval for use, any application or system that records PII (for example, a smartphone data collection app or a database) must be evaluated with respect to its potential impact on privacy by means of a PIA.

USGS Tweet Earthquake Dispatch (@USGSted): Using Twitter for Earthquake Detection and Characterization
Paul Earle, Geophysicist, USGS National Earthquake Information Center; and Sophia Liu, Mendenhall USGS Research Fellow, National Earthquake Information Center
http://twitter.com/USGSted
http://twitter.com/USGSBigQuakes

The USGS is investigating how online social networking services like Twitter—a microblogging service for sending and reading public text-based messages of up to 140 characters—can augment USGS earthquake response products and the delivery of hazard information. The USGS TED system is using Twitter not only to broadcast seismically verified earthquake alerts via the @USGSted and @USGSbigquakes Twitter accounts, but also to rapidly detect widely felt seismic events through a real-time detection system.

The detector algorithm scans for significant increases in tweets containing the word "earthquake" or its equivalent in other languages and sends internal alerts with the detection time, tweet text, and the location of the city where most of the tweets originated. It has been running in real-time for 7 months and finds, on average, two or three felt events per day with a false detection rate of less than 10 percent. The detections have reasonable coverage of populated areas worldwide. The number of detections is small compared to the number of earthquakes detected seismically, and only a rough location and qualitative assessment of shaking can be determined based on Tweet data alone. However, the Twitter detections are generally caused by widely felt events that are of more immediate interest than those with no human impact. The main benefit of the tweet-based detections is speed, with most detections occurring between 19 seconds and 2 minutes from the origin time. This is considerably faster than seismic detections in poorly instrumented regions of the world.

Going beyond the initial detection, the USGS is developing data mining techniques to continuously archive and analyze relevant tweets for additional details about the detected events. The information generated about an event is displayed on an internal Web-based map designed using HTML5 for the mobile environment, which can be valuable when the user is not able to access a desktop computer at the time of the detections. Future additions (for example, seismograms, time series of tweets-per-minute, word clouds, recently uploaded earthquake photos, and so forth) are being investigated to provide a more in-depth characterization of the seismic events based on an analysis of tweet text and content from other social media sources.

An Overview of the USGS Nonindigenous Aquatic Species (NAS) Online Sighting Report System and Lessons Learned from Mobile App Development
Matthew Cannister, Biological Technician, USGS Southeast Ecological Science Center

The USGS NAS database is a collection of georeferenced accounts of introduced aquatic species. This presentation will focus on the online Sighting Report Form, a tool provided on the NAS Web site (*http://nas.er.usgs.gov*) that provides an easy method for visitors to report a nonnative species observation. Finally, I will briefly outline our experiences with the production of a mobile app designed to provide a more convenient way to report species occurrences.

Engaging the Public in Scientific Research Perspectives from the Volunteer Monitoring Community
Barb Horn, Water Resource Specialist, Colorado Parks and Wildlife
http://www.rivernetwork.org/
http://wildlife.state.co.us/LandWater/Riverwatch/Pages/Riverwatch.aspx
http://acwi.gov/monitoring/vm/index.html
https://lists.uwex.edu/mailman/listinfo/extvolmonnet
http://www.usawaterquality.org/volunteer/
http://water.epa.gov/type/rsl/monitoring/listinstruct.cfm
http://www.coloradowater.org/

The water-quality Volunteer Monitoring (VM) community has a 50-plus-year history. The community has grown over time from east to the west across the Nation, as has its efforts: from monitoring in lakes now expanding to streams, large rivers, groundwater, estuaries and oceans; from chemical indicators to monitoring physical habitat, biological, flow, and geomorphology (as examples) indicators; and from water into wetlands, riparian zones, sediment, and other habitat monitoring. The movement has grown from small grass roots groups to large and effective networks. This vast, diverse, and successful community attempts to share their successes, resources, and challenges.

This presentation will provide the VM community perspective on engaging the public in research and other data uses. Topics covered will also include how to find information and groups, discuss key program elements to support volunteers, how to achieve measurable results using volunteers, and suggest organizational and program approaches and tips on effective volunteer management. An update will be provided for the nearly new effort looking at the use of volunteers in the USGS NAWQA Program. VM is not free, but can be extremely cost-effective if implemented appropriately.

The Evolving Landscape of Citizen Science: Typologies and Implications of Project Design
Andrea Wiggins, Postdoctoral Fellow, Cornell Lab of Ornithology

Public participation in scientific research encompasses a surprisingly broad and continually evolving variety of goals and structures. The terminology and typologies associated with these practices provide insight into the advantages and disadvantages of these approaches and associated goals. This talk will begin with an overview of labels, typologies, and related practices in this field. The pros and cons of different forms of citizen science will be discussed from several angles, including participation, information technologies, data, and sustainability.

CitSci.org: Cyberinfrastructure Support for Grassroots Conservation, Citizen Science, and Community-Based Monitoring
Greg Newman, Ecologist/Web Designer, Colorado State University

Citizen science and community-based monitoring conservation programs are increasing in number and breadth, generating volumes of scientific data. Many programs are ill-equipped to effectively manage these data. We built a cyberinfrastructure support system for citizen science programs (www.citsci.org) to support the spectrum of program management and data management needs. The system affords program coordinators the opportunity to create their own projects, manage project members, build their own data entry sheets, streamline data entry, visualize data on maps, automate custom analyses, and get feedback. Thus far, CitSci.org has engaged 34 programs resulting in some 7,000+ natural resource observations. The majority of programs are grassroots efforts with conservation biology-oriented goals and objectives. For example, the Front Range Pika Project engages citizen scientists in conservation research on the American pika (Ochotona princeps). Volunteers follow protocols to collect data about pikas and their habitat in high-altitude sites, thereby assessing the impacts of climate change on pika populations. Here, we discuss the unique opportunities afforded by CitSci.org to support the needs of citizen science, community-based monitoring, and grassroots conservation biology programs within the USGS to connect people, nature, research, and education.

Volunteer Map Data Collection - The National Map Corps
Greg Matthews, Project Manager The National Map Corps, USGS National Geospatial Technical Operation Center
https://my.usgs.gov/confluence/display/nationalmapcorps/Home

The National Map Corps is a USGS project to collect and manage Volunteered Geographic Information (VGI). Because of the changing technical landscape, the increasing use of social media for citizen mapping, and mandates for more transparency and citizen involvement in Government, the USGS is investigating the redefinition of its volunteer program. Since 1994, the USGS has involved citizens in processes to improve topographic maps. In 2010, the Open Street Map Collaborative Project (OSMCP) was started to evaluate the suitability of using an existing Web-based collection system for data contributions and improvements by partnering with a State agency to update roads data using common specifications and editing guidelines. The first phase of the project demonstrated a successful deployment of the OpenStreetMap (OSM) Potlatch editor, customized with USGS specifications, to allow multiple editors to successfully edit roads data for part of Kansas.

In 2011, Phase Two of the OSMCP focused on student volunteer collection of 30 structure types defined as part of The National Map. Because Phase Two of the project involved a wider, less-formal group of volunteers, attention was paid to elements of the editing interface to ensure that it more closely complied with USGS data collection specifications for structures. Change detection was implemented throughout this phase and quality metrics were created.

The current phase of this project, Phase Three, follows the concepts laid out in Phase Two for collecting structures. Phase Three has expanded the focus of the project across the entire State of Colorado.

Once the effectiveness of the volunteer data collection process can be analyzed, the program may expand nationwide.

Contact: Greg Matthews Nationalmapcorps@usgs.gov

The Alaska Volcano Observatory Citizen Network Ash Collection and Observation Program
Kristi Wallace, Geologist, USGS Alaska Volcano Observatory
http://www.avo.alaska.edu/ashreport.php
http://www.avo.alaska.edu/ashreports/report_map.php

The remoteness of many of Alaska's 52 historically active volcanoes makes direct eruption observations and real-time ash-fall collection challenging. As a result, scientists at the Alaska Volcano Observatory (AVO) ask citizens positioned both near active volcanoes and under the path of eruption clouds to make voluntary observations and collect ash samples during eruptions. Scientists at AVO make these requests to individuals by phone, postal, and electronic mailings, and advertise the need more broadly on the AVO Web site. AVO provides detailed instructions for making observations and collecting samples as online documents and as a video; both can be mailed to communities without Internet access. In addition, AVO has held community workshops to educate volunteer observers and provide collection materials (tools and mailers). Because of the varied abilities and interests of the general public and environmental conditions, AVO provides instructions for a variety of acceptable collection procedures. Observations can be submitted directly to AVO's database-driven Web site, or by phone, mail, or hand delivery. A recently developed Web-based geographic interface helps scientists to visualize the locations of ash-fall activity in near real time. During the 2009 eruption of Redoubt volcano, AVO received approximately 250 written or verbal observations and 55 physical samples from the public, including time-incremental collections during prolonged ash-fall events; measured-area samples, and bulk samples. Timely posting of eruption and ash-fall information improves the accuracy of official warning messages and thus the effectiveness of communicating volcano hazards information to the public. Observations of ash-fall events, including timing, location, and amount, are communicated directly to the National Weather Service so that public ash-fall advisory statements can be updated. Scientists use ash-fall samples and observations to understand the composition, volume, and dispersal pattern of the ash clouds.

Data Management for Citizen Science: Challenges and Opportunities for USGS Leadership
Andrea Wiggins, Postdoctoral Fellow, Cornell Lab of Ornithology

Data management is an area of growing concern across the sciences. This talk begins with an overview of data management issues in citizen science from the standpoint of the data life cycle, with an introduction to the DataONE Public Participation in Scientific Research Working Group's current projects and future plans. A brief summary of recent survey results on data management satisfaction and needs based on responses from citizen science projects funded by governmental agencies prefaces a discussion of the high-level challenges currently facing citizen science data managers. These topics include issues related to policy, cyberinfrastructure and technologies, perceptions of data quality, and the disconnect between short-term priorities and long-term data management realities—all of which have cascading effects on many other aspects of data management. The talk concludes with a summary of areas in which citizen science projects in governmental agencies can lead the way in citizen science by developing community capacity and demonstrating excellence in data management.

Public Participation in the Digitization of Biodiversity Collections
Austin Mast, Associate Professor, Florida State University
https://www.idigbio.org/

There are approximately 1 billion biodiversity research specimens in the United States, with information pertaining to as few as 10 percent of them available online at present. Recently, the community has mobilized around the goal of digitizing a large portion of the remaining 900 million specimens in the next 10 years. This will require greater interinstitutional collaboration and improved cyberinfrastructure, as well as broader public participation. I will introduce iDigBio (the National Resource for Advancing Digitization of Biodiversity Collections) and the thematic collections networks, projects funded by NSF's Advancing Digitization of Biodiversity Collections program. iDigBio will host a workshop on public participation in digitization later this month, and I will introduce the ways I anticipate that the public can contribute significantly to specimen curation and imaging, text transcription, and specimen description (for example, specimen flowering or not) from images, and georeferencing.

Social.Water and CrowdHydrology
Michael Fienen, Research Hydrologist, USGS Wisconsin Water Science Center

Remote telemetry has a long history at USGS and other hydrologic monitoring organizations, enabling real-time hydrologic data presentation on the Web. Citizen volunteers have also long contributed to hydrologic data collection. Today, the opportunity exists to combine these two ways of collecting information. Ubiquitous text messaging and email-capable mobile phones mean nearly everyone can provide telemetric data if they know what information to provide and if the infrastructure to accept the information exists: this is "crowdsourcing."

Crowdhydrology.org, a crowdsourcing project in New York, was implemented by posting signs near stream staff gages inviting passersby to send text messages reporting the value they read on the gage. Social.Water is a tool developed to automatically accept and interpret these messages, generate data tables and graphical results, and post them on the Web. Social.Water was written using open-source codes and protocols for reading and interpreting text messages that were forwarded to an email account and ultimately used to update a database. Results are also reported to the Web in near real time. Initial validation with conventional techniques shows favorable quality of crowdsourced data.

Framework for Public Participation GIS: Options for Federal Agencies
Tim Kern, Computer Engineer, USGS Fort Collins Science Center

Public participation in resource mapping is nothing new. Local authorities have long convened meetings with residents to identify areas of critical interest to the community. What separates these efforts from current practices is the multitude of methods that can be employed to capture and share spatial inputs from the public.

This presentation will discuss a USGS-developed framework for public geospatial data collection that employs a number of current data capture and display techniques. This framework includes ways to define a study area and prepare a mission-specific view, the various data collection options available to the user, submission concerns and approaches, data validation, data life-cycle management, and the trauma associated with public data collection by a Federal agency.

The U.S. Forest Service currently uses this framework to map areas of concern, as well as capture discoveries (species observations, habitat disconnects, and disturbance issues) in various national forests. A pilot project, focused on Chugach National Forest, allowed us to explore and develop the technical, security, quality-assurance, and data management aspects of the framework.

Citizen Science—Data Management: A Vision for the Future
Derek Masaki, Biological Data Manager/Geospatial Liaison, Core Science Analytics and Synthesis

At the 2012 Techcrunch conference in New York City, Todd Park, Federal Chief Technical Officer, remarked, "We want to disrupt the U.S. Government and we want your help." Innovation-driven transformation has been disruptive to media, communication, and education. The platform outlined in the President's "Digital Government Strategy" unveiled at the TechCrunch event indicates that technology-led disruption is coming to Federal agencies now, too.

Citizen science is a key inroad to bringing new methods, technology, and participation to the halls of the government science agencies in the United States. Few other emerging trends are better suited to embrace the "open, social, mobile" aspects of the Federal digital government initiative.

Derek Masaki, with USGS, will provide an introduction to emerging technology trends in citizen science, demonstrate why we should stop loathing and start loving volunteered science data, and, finally, provide a framework for dealing with the oncoming flood of data coming our way.

The Encyclopedia of Life as a Source of Materials and a Venue for Showing off Your Work
Jen Hammock, Coordinator, Encyclopedia of Life
http://eol.org/data_objects/17769157
http://eol.org/data_objects/15631926
http://www.inaturalist.org/
http://www.morphbank.net/
http://eol.org/info/82
http://www.eol.org
http://www.diveboard.com/
http://eol.org/api
http://scratchpads.eu/
http://eol.org/info/cp_getting_started
http://www.flickr.com/groups/encyclopedia_of_life/pool
http://fieldguides.eol.org/

There are a number of ways in which the Encyclopedia of Life (EOL) can collaborate with citizen science projects and programs in biology. The EOL open-access collection of multimedia, references, and descriptive text is freely available for projects developing training, education, and outreach materials. This content can be selected by hand or delivered automatically to a partner Web site by EOL's Web services.

Citizen Science projects can also publish their work on EOL if they wish to disseminate it widely under a Creative Commons license. Connectors are already in place for two partner platforms that accept individually contributed wildlife images, and several more connectors are in development. Content displayed on EOL will be linked back to the partner's Web site and partners also have access to traffic statistics to their content on EOL.

A number of online repositories for various kinds of biodiversity information are sharing their holdings with EOL. Some of these provide services that EOL does not (for example, bulk image upload) as well as an additional venue and corresponding audience for the shared content.

Examples of existing content use cases and content sharing will be presented as well as pointers to online documentation for both contributing and consuming content. Time will be reserved for questions.

Jen Hammock was once a chemist, completed her doctorate in biology at Woods Hole Oceanographic Institution, and is currently with the Species Pages Group at EOL; her responsibilities include working with partner projects, either contributing or utilizing content on the EOL platform. She loves to dive.

The North American Bird Phenlology Program: Reviving a Historic Program in the Digital Age
Jessica Zelt, Program Coordinator, USGS Patuxent Wildlife Research Center

Patuxent Wildlife Research Center is home to several historic databases of value, including the North American Bird Phenology Program (BPP). We describe the origin and historic use of the dataset, recent use, and potential uses and value. The BPP originated in the late 1800s and continued into the mid-1900s. The BPP started as observations on bird migration reported by observers, and the continued collection and organization of these data became the impetus for the American Ornithologists' Union to successfully lobby for the formation of the Economic Ornithology program. Government biologists published from these sources through the early 1900s, but the material became largely neglected after mid-century. The current urgency of documenting phenology and global climate change, combined with technological advancement, has created important opportunities for new uses of this dataset. We discuss recent and ongoing projects, and opportunities for the scientific community to use, help preserve, and increase access to these important resources.

2012 Baltimore/DC Cricket Crawl—Counting Insects With Cellphones
Derek Masaki, Biological Data Manager/Geospatial Liaison, Core Science Analytics and Synthesis

On August 24, 2012, citizen scientists, artists, naturalists and casual participants were invited to join an evening sound census of the late summer crickets and katydids singing throughout the Baltimore/D.C. metro areas. Those participating in the "crawl" were encouraged to use social media, email, and text messages on their mobile devices to report locations of the eight target species.

The event extended the efforts of the original 2009 New York City Cricket Crawl where 300 volunteers, assisted by USGS biologists, used their cellphones to survey for native crickets and katydids in the heart of America's most populous city. The teams found all seven targeted species and provided new occurrence points for an insect group last surveyed in New York over 100 years ago.

Sam Droege and Derek Masaki, with USGS, will lead a discussion on the methods used in the survey, review outcomes, and provide guidance on conducting a survey in your neighborhood.

Discover Life: Networking Study Sites to Predict the Impact of Climate Change and Other Factors on Species and Their Interactions
John Pickering, Associate Professor, University of Georgia; Developer, DiscoverLife

Let's enable teachers and their students to run a network of ecological research sites around the world, engage them and their communities in science, and generate the knowledge that society needs to understand and address pressing environmental issues.

Discover Life (www.discoverlife.org) provides online tools and research protocols for scientists and the public to collect and analyze high-quality data on species and their interactions. These tools include photographic albums, identification guides, a global mapper, and automated analysis software. The talk will focus on Discover Life's Mothing project (*http://www.discoverlife.org/moth*), the primary goal of which is to document how weather, latitude, and land use affect the diversity, phenology, and abundance of moths. Since 2010, participants have submitted over 100,000 photographs of moths and other creatures attracted to lights at sites in the United States and Costa Rica. It will describe how species are identified and data processed nightly. Examples will show seasonal differences in diversity, abundance, and number of generations through time and at different latitudes.

Women in Technology/STEMworks—Mobilizing K–12 Student Scientists
Isla Young, Director K–12 STEM Education, Women in Technology, Maui Economic Development Board

The integration of Science, Technology, Engineering, and Mathematics (STEM) and Service Learning into K–12 STEM education demands creativity and persistence (Nielsen and others, 2011; Demirci, 2011; Breetzke and others, 2011). This presentation will use Maui Economic Development Board, Women in Technology Project's STEMworks—a project-based, service-learning oriented program that provides students with the most current, high-end technologies available in some of the most progressive fields in the world Computer Aided Design (CAD), Animation, GIS, GPS, Softimage, Game Design, Web site Design, app development, and so forth). STEMworks attempts to cultivate and nurture a series of relationships with the goal of providing students the opportunity to engage in self-directed, team, and project-based STEM service-learning projects that contribute to the wider community in which they live, study, and play. STEMworks outreach is especially suited to reach large numbers of students with its equity-centric, place-based, cultural approach that fosters the participation of various underrepresented groups in STEM education, especially women and native Hawaiians. STEMworks' close collaboration and partnerships with USGS, ESRI, National Geographic, Google, Hawaii Geographic Information Coordinating Council, and other organizations will also be discussed.

Appendix C.   Posters

The Current Landscape of Public Participation in USGS Science
Sally L. Holl, U. S. Geological Survey
Megan K. Hines, University of Wisconsin – Madison, Wis.

Volunteers have an established role in USGS science. USGS records contain volunteer information dating back to the late 1800s when, for example, citizen volunteers monitored streamflow. The public continues to participate in programs such as Did You Feel It?, Nature's Notebook, and the North American Breeding Bird Survey. Recently, two broad-based efforts related to citizen science have been initiated. First, a CSWG formed within the USGS CDI in August of 2011. An interdisciplinary group of USGS scientists and partners now meet regularly to promote an understanding of the roles and outcomes of citizen science in the conduct of USGS research, to facilitate and enhance connections between the USGS and the citizen science community, to provide access to information and tools to support the effective use of citizen science data in the USGS, and to engage the public in USGS science and improve scientific literacy. Second, the Applied Earth Systems Informatics Research (AESIR) group was recently established within the USGS CSS mission area. AESIR, in collaboration with the CSWG and other CDI groups, is devoting resources to answering high-level research questions regarding cyberinfrastructure and informatics to support citizen science.

Improving Access to Water Information: The NWIS Web Services Snapshot
Sally L. Holl, U.S. Geological Survey

The NWIS Web Services Snapshot Tool for ArcGIS enables rapid access to the USGS National Water Information System (NWIS), a database containing hydrologic information for more than 1.5 million surface-water, groundwater, and atmospheric monitoring sites throughout the United States, some with a record of more than 100 years. NWIS data are considered the gold standard of hydrologic information and are accessed daily by the public.

The Snapshot Tool is an ArcMap add-in that allows users to query NWIS Web Services, which provide site information, water-quality, instantaneous streamflow, and daily streamflow measurements, and retrieve a snapshot (subset) of the data to a local personal geodatabase. The relational structure of the geodatabase and added convenience functionality, such as domains, eliminate the laborious process of reconstructing a workable geodatabase and interpreting database codes, thus allowing a user to immediately begin working with the data.

Year One of a Citizen Science Monitoring Network: Lake Michigan Volunteer AMBLE
Jennifer G. Chipault,[1] C. LeAnn White,[1] Sue Jennings,[2] Emily H. Tyner,[2] and Marne L. Kaeske[3]

[1]U.S. Geological Survey's National Wildlife Health Center, Madison, Wisconsin

[2]National Park Service's Sleeping Bear Dunes National Lakeshore, Empire, Michigan

[3]The Ridges Sanctuary, Baileys Harbor, Wisconsin

Bird mortality caused by ingestion of a toxin produced by the bacterium Clostridium botulinum has been periodically reported on the Great Lakes since the 1960s. Resurgence of avian botulism outbreaks since the late 1990s has brought renewed attention to this wildlife health issue. As part of the Great Lakes Restoration Initiative, a citizen science program called Lake Michigan Volunteer AMBLE (Avian Monitoring for Botulism Lakeshore Events) began in Door County, Wis., in 2011. AMBLE volunteers walked designated sections of lakeshore weekly from June through November, collecting data on species and numbers of healthy, sick, and dead birds observed. Forty-four trained volunteers covered 17 miles of transects in Door County during the 2011 monitoring season. Five sick and 82 dead birds were reported. A subset (21) of the carcasses found in Door County was tested for botulinum toxin at the USGS National Wildlife Health Center; 12 were confirmed to have avian botulism type E. The AMBLE program continues in Door County in 2012 and has expanded around Green Bay, Wis. A network of citizen scientists can consistently monitor a broad geographic area, providing valuable data on avian botulism trends, and increasing the chances of detecting a wildlife mortality event.

Appendix D.   Workshop Agenda

Citizen Science Workshop

September 11–12, 2012, Denver Federal Center, Bldg. 810, Ice Core Auditorium

Day 1—September 11, 2012

Opening and Welcome		**Megan Hines and Abby Benson**
8:00	Introductions and Logistics	Megan Hines, University of Wisconsin, Madison
8:00–8:05	Welcome to Denver	Randy Updike, Regional Executive for the Rocky Mountain Area
8:05–8:20	Welcome to the CDI Citizen Science Workshop	Linda Gundersen, Director, Office of Workshop Science Quality and Integrity
8:20–8:40	Exploring the Landscape of Citizen Science	Jennifer Shirk, Cornell Lab of and Public Participation in Scientific Research Ornithology (W)

Citizen Science Policy and Challenges		**Annie Simpson**
8:40–8:45	Introduction	Annie Simpson, USGS Biologist and Information Scientist
8:45–9:00	Ensuring Legal and Policy Compliant	Lorna Schmid, USGS Infrastructure Citizen Science App Development and Operations Team Lead
9:00–9:15	Researcher Point of View: iPlover: A Smartphone Application to Characterize Piping Plover Nest Locations	Rob Thieler, USGS Research Scientist
9:15–9:30	USGS Volunteer Program and Handbook	Cheryl Smith, USGS Volunteer Program Coordinator (W)
9:30–9:45	Researcher Point of View: How are USGS Citizen Science Projects Impacted by Government Policies?	Eric Wolf, USGS and Barbara Poore, USGS Center for Coastal and Watershed Studies
9:45–10:15	**BREAK**	
10:15–10:20	Three Laws Impacting Science Activities	Shari Baloch and David Newman, Office of Enterprise Information (W)
10:20–10:25	Researcher Point of View: USGS Tweet Earthquake Dispatch (@USGSted): Using Twitter for Earthquake Detection and Characterization	Paul Earle, USGS Research Geographer
10:25–10:50	Welcome to the CDI Citizen Science Workshop	Kevin Gallagher, Associate Director, Core Science Systems
10:50–11:00	Researcher Point of View: An Overview of the USGS Nonindigenous Aquatic Species (NAS) Online Sighting Report System and Lessons Learned from Mobile App Development	Matt Cannister, USGS Biological Technician

11:00–12:00	Structured Discussion	All
12:00–1:00	**LUNCH**	

Engaging the Public in Scientific Research		**Barbara Poore and Dave Govoni**
1:00–1:05	Introduction	Barbara Poore, USGS Center for Coastal and Watershed Studies
1:05–1:25	Engaging the Public in Scientific Research Perspectives from the Volunteer Monitoring Community	Barb Horn, State of Colorado (W)
1:25–1:45	The Evolving Landscape of Citizen Science: Typologies and Implications of Project Design	Andrea Wiggins, Cornell Lab of Ornithology/DataONE
1:45–2:05	CitSci.org: Cyberinfrastructure Support for Grassroots Conservation, Citizen Science, and Community-Based Monitoring	Greg Newman, Colorado State University
2:05–2:20	**BREAK**	
2:20–2:40	Volunteer Map Data Collection—The National Maps Corps	Greg Matthews, USGS National Map Corps
2:40–3:00	The Alaskan Volcano Observatory Citizen Network Ash Collection and Observation Program	Kristi Wallace, USGS Alaska Volcano Observatory
3:00–4:00	Structured Discussion	All

Day 2—September 12, 2012

Data Collection and Management		**Megan Hines and Steve Tessler**
8:00–8:10	Day 1 Summary and Logistics	Steve Tessler, USGS Ecologist and Data Manager
8:10–8:30	Data Management for Citizen Science: Challenges and Opportunities for USGS Leadership	Andrea Wiggins, Cornell Lab of Ornithology/DataONE
8:30–8:50	Public Participation in the Digitization of Biodiversity Collections	Austin Mast, Florida State University, iDigBio
8:50–9:10	Social.Water and CrowdHydrology	Mike Fienen, USGS Wisconsin Water Science Center
9:10–9:40	**BREAK**	
9:40–10:00	Public Participation in GIS Tools Supporting Citizen Science Data Collection, and New Citizen Science Efforts Beginning	Tim Kern, USGS Fort Collins Science Center
10:00–10:20	Citizen Science—Data Management: A Vision for the Future	Derek Masaki, USGS
10:20–11:20	Structured Discussion	All
11:20–12:30	**LUNCH**	

Technology and Tools		**Derek Masaki**

12:30–12:45	Introduction	Derek Masaki, USGS
12:45–1:05	The Encyclopedia of Life as a Source of Materials and a Venue for Showing Off Your Work	Jen Hammock, Encyclopedia of Life (W)
1:05–1:25	The North American Bird Phenology Program:Reviving a Historic Program in the Digital Age	Jessica Zelt, USGS Patuxent Wildlife Research Center
1:25–1:45	2012 Baltimore/DC Cricket Crawl—Counting Insects with Cellphones	Derek Masaki, USGS
1:45–2:20	**BREAK**	
2:20–2:40	Discover Life—Networking Study Sites to Predict the Impact of Climate Change and Other Factors on Species and Their Interactions	John Pickering, Discover Life
2:40–3:00	Women in Technology/STEMworks— Mobilizing K–12 Student Scientists	Isla Young, Maui Economic Development Board
3:00–4:00	Structured Discussion	All
6:00	**Dinner Out**	

*(W) indicates presentation via WebEx.

Appendix E.   Meeting Handouts

The Art and Science of Multi-Scale Citizen Science Support
Newman, G., Graham, J., Crall, A., and Laituri, M., 2011, v. 6, no. 3–4, p. 217–227, doi: 10.1016/j.ecoinf.2011.03.002.

   Citizen science and community-based monitoring programs are increasing in number and breadth, generating volumes of scientific data. Many programs are ill-equipped to effectively manage these data. We examined the art and science of multi-scale citizen science support, focusing on issues of integration and flexibility that arise for data management when programs span multiple spatial, temporal, and social scales across many domains. Our objectives were to: (1) briefly review existing citizen science approaches and data management needs; (2) propose a framework for multi-scale citizen science support; (3) develop a cyberinfrastructure to support citizen science program needs; and (4) describe lessons learned. We find that approaches differ in scope, scale, and activities and that the proposed framework situates programs while guiding cyberinfrastructure system development. We built a cyberinfrastructure support system for citizen science programs (_www.citsci.org_) and showed that carefully designed systems can be adept enough to support programs at multiple spatial and temporal scales across many domains when built with a flexible architecture. The advantage of a flexible, yet controlled, cyberinfrastructure system lies in the ability of users with different levels of permission to easily customize the features themselves, while adhering to controlled vocabularies necessary for cross-discipline comparisons and meta-analyses. Program evaluation tied to this framework and integrated into cyberinfrastructure support systems will improve our ability to track effectiveness. We compare existing systems and discuss the importance of standards for interoperability and the challenges associated with system maintenance and long-term support. We conclude by offering a vision of the future of citizen science data management and cyberinfrastructure support.

Freedom of Information Act—Employee Responsibilities
Newman, D.J., 2012, Freedom of Information Act—Employee responsibilities: U.S. Geological Survey General Interest Product 140, 2 p. (_http://pubs.usgs.gov/gip/140_)

   The FOIA, 5 U.S.C. § 552, as amended, generally provides that any person has a right to request access to Federal agency records. The USGS proactively promotes information disclosure as inherent to its mission of providing objective science to inform decisionmakers and the general public. USGS scientists disseminate up-to-date and historical scientific data that are critical to addressing national and global priorities.

The Future of Citizen Science: Emerging Technologies and Shifting Paradigms
Newman, G., Wiggins, A., Crall, A., Graham, E., Newman, S., and Crowston, K., 2012, Frontiers in Ecology and the Environment, v. 10, no. 6, p. 298-304, doi: 10.1890/110294.

   Citizen science creates a nexus between science and education that, when coupled with emerging technologies, expands the frontiers of ecological research and public engagement. Using representative technologies and other examples, we examine the future of citizen science in terms of its research processes, program and participant cultures, and scientific communities. Future citizen science projects will likely be influenced by sociocultural issues related to new technologies and will continue to face practical programmatic challenges. We foresee networked, open science and the use of online computer/video gaming as important tools to engage nontraditional audiences, and offer recommendations to help prepare project managers for impending challenges. A more formalized citizen science enterprise, complete with networked organizations, associations, journals, and cyberinfrastructure, will advance scientific research, including ecology, and further public education.

Read More: _http://www.esajournals.org/doi/abs/10.1890/110294_

A

SCIENCE IN COMPLIANCE:
WHAT YOU NEED TO KNOW ABOUT COLLECTING INFORMATION

Interested in conducting a telephone survey?
Would you like to solicit information from your industry?
Want to create a survey or a form for public use?
If you answered "yes" to any of the above questions, please read on!

The **Paperwork Reduction Act of 1995 (PRA)** requires agencies to acquire OMB approval before collecting the structured information from 10 or more members of the public annually.	"**Public**" includes: individuals, partnerships, corporations, universities, nonprofit organizations, State, local, and tribal governments and agencies, and other associations and organizations, whether foreign or domestic. Federal agencies are not included.

What's the Point?
The PRA was enacted to minimize the burden that the Government imposes on the public and improve the quality and use of Federal information.

Examples of a **structured information collection** could be a form, a Web-page survey, a regulatory requirement to provide certain information, or a telephone survey set of questions.	**Office of Management and Budget (OMB)** clearance is not required to collect information from other Federal agencies, unless the information will be used for general statistical purposes.

Agreements and the PRA

- For grants, there is usually very little Federal involvement in the data collection. Therefore, PRA review and clearance may not be needed; however, there are exceptions. For example, if the Federal Government specifies a standard reporting mechanism for the grantees, PRA clearance would be required.

- For cooperative agreements, PRA review and approval is required if the USGS office has significant input/control into the design, methodology, and analysis of the data collection or if the data is stored at the USGS Office level. The reason is that the need for PRA clearance is dependent on the level of control the Government has over the collection.

- For contracts, the USGS has complete responsibility for the data and data collections procedures. The USGS owns the data and it is stored at the program office. Therefore, all data collections performed under contracts need PRA clearance. A collection conducted by a State agency needs clearance if USGS is specifically paying the State to conduct a collection or if the USGS must approve a data collection instrument (for example, a form).

What is the process?

Generally,

1. Science or administrative program office develops or revises the actual information collection instrument.

2. Program office publishes 60-day Federal Register notice proposing the collection.

3. Program office prepares paperwork for submission.

4. Program office submits paperwork package to USGS Information Collection Clearance Officer (ICCO) for review.

5. USGS ICCO submits package to DOI ICCO for approval.

6. After approval from DOI, program office publishes a 30-day Federal Register notice telling public we are sending request to OMB.

7. DOI ICCO submits request to OMB.

8. OMB will review and respond with approval after 60 days.

How long does it take to complete the process?
The complete review and approval process can take anywhere from 6 to 9 months. This estimate includes the 60-day and 30-day public comment periods and the 60 days OMB has to review and act upon each submission.

Figure 1. Handout prepared by Shari Baloch (USGS) and distributed at the first U.S. Geological Survey Citizen Science Workshop, held in Denver, Colo., September 11–13, 2012. The handout, "Science In Compliance; What You Need to Know about Collecting Information," has (*A*) a page of guidelines and procedures and (*B*) a page of frequently asked questions.

B

FAQs	
Can a data collection be conducted without PRA approval if fewer than 10 respondents are involved?	Yes; the PRA only applies to collections directed at 10 or more persons.
Does the PRA affect questions at public meetings?	Not usually. Clearance is not needed if the attendees are just asked to comment or give suggestions on the program or subject in question. If, however, the group is gathered for the purpose of having attendees respond to a specific set of formatted questions, then the PRA **does** apply.
Do you need PRA clearance if you just ask people for comments on a document or public comments through the Federal Register?	A PRA clearance is not necessary unless respondents are asked to answer specific questions in their comments. If the comment is very general, the PRA does not apply.
Does the PRA affect surveys on the Web?	Yes, with the exception that PRA clearance is not necessary for very general invitations for public comments and suggestions. The PRA **does** apply if specific, structured questions are asked or if a form is used for the information collection.
Do you need PRA clearance if the respondents are foreigners or foreign governments?	You need to obtain clearance for any information you gather from foreign citizens or companies. You do not need clearance for information submitted by a foreign government, with one caveat: If a foreign government is required to gather information from its citizens to meet a U.S. requirement (that is, passports), then PRA clearance is needed.
Is there any way for OMB to grant an emergency approval?	There are provisions in the PRA for emergency processing of Internal Collection Review packages. Approvals obtained this way are only good for a maximum of 6 months, allowing enough time to obtain approval through the normal process, if necessary. Emergency processing is only to be used to respond to circumstances that could not be foreseen and when the use of regular procedures would result in significant harm to the public or the program. Failure to plan, avoidance of embarrassment, and so forth, are not valid justifications. Requests for emergency processing must be approved in advance by the OMB Desk Officer.
What is a "Generic" Information Collection Request?	A Generic Information Collection, also known as a generic clearance, obtains OMB approval for a master plan for a number of similar surveys that have the same general purpose (for example, customer surveys). Individual surveys conducted under the clearance are reviewed by OMB on a fast-track basis and the process involves less documentation. Generic clearances provide more flexibility for certain types of surveys, but they can be harder to track and are not appropriate for many types of information collection efforts.
What happens if a program office is already collecting information from the public without OMB approval?	The PRA is a law and failure to comply with the requirements of the Act is breaking the law. The Chief Information Officer is the senior policy official responsible for compliance with the law. When OMB becomes aware of a PRA violation, it is brought to the CIO's attention. If the violation is not resolved in a timely manner, the issue is raised in OMB's management chain and can result in official Departmental reprimands and may have budget implications.
Can social media tools be used in lieu of an Information Collection?	Under the PRA, facts or opinions obtained in connection with public meetings do not count as "information." This "public meeting" exception allows agencies to engage with the public on the Internet as long as the engagement is the functional equivalent of a public meeting (that is, not a survey). In addition, it is important to underline that general solicitations, such as Federal Register notices, do not trigger the PRA. It follows that agencies may offer the public opportunities to provide general comments on discussion topics through the Internet. More generally, agencies may use social media and Web-based technologies in a variety of specific ways without triggering the PRA. Notably, OMB's regulations implementing the PRA exclude facts or opinions provided in response to general solicitations published in the Federal Register or other publications. Any information collection that will use social media tools should be coordinated with the Information Collection Clearance Officer during the planning phase.
Additional Resources	
USGS Information Collections Web site: *http://internal.usgs.gov/gio/irm/info.html* OMB Office of Information and Regulatory Affairs: *http://www.whitehouse.gov/omb/inforeg_infocoll* PRA: *http://www.archives.gov/federal-register/laws/paperwork-reduction/*	

Figure 1.   Handout prepared by Shari Baloch (USGS) and distributed at the first U.S. Geological Survey Citizen Science Workshop, held in Denver, Colo., September 11–13, 2012. The handout, "Science In Compliance; What You Need to Know about Collecting Information," has (*A*) a page of guidelines and procedures and (*B*) a page of frequently asked questions.—Continued

Integration and Dissemination of Citizen Reported and Seismically Derived Earthquake Information via Social Network Technologies
Guy, M., Earle, P., Ostrum, C., Gruchalla, K., and Horvath, S., 2010, Lecture Notes in Computer Science, v. 6065, p. 42–53, doi: 10.1007/978-3-642-13062-5_6.

   People in the locality of earthquakes are publishing anecdotal information about the shaking within seconds of their occurrences via social network technologies, such as Twitter. In contrast, depending on the size and location of the earthquake, scientific alerts can take between 2 to 20 minutes to publish. We describe Tweet Earthquake Dispatch (TED)—a system that adopts social network technologies to augment earthquake response products and the delivery of hazard information. The TED system analyzes data from these social networks for multiple purposes: (1) to integrate citizen reports of earthquakes with corresponding scientific reports; (2) to infer the public level of interest in an earthquake for tailoring outputs disseminated via social network technologies; and (3) to explore the possibility of rapid detection of a probable earthquake, within seconds of its occurrence, helping to fill the gap between the earthquake origin time and the presence of quantitative scientific data.

North American Bird Phenology Program
Zelt, J., 2008, Unpublished handout.
http://www.pwrc.usgs.gov/products/factsheets/bpp_factsheetsm.pdf

   The USGS houses a unique and largely forgotten collection of approximately 6,000,000 migration cards that illuminate migration patterns and population status of birds in North America. These handwritten cards contain almost all of what was known of bird distribution and migration from the late 17th century to the later part of the 19th century. The bulk of the records are the result of a network of observers who recorded migration arrival dates in the spring and fall that, at its height, involved over 3,000 participants. In 2009, those records were resurrected from the basements of Patuxent Wildlife Research Center and turned into a dynamic citizen science program called the North American Bird Phenology Program (BPP). The BPP relies on a worldwide network of over 2,500 volunteers to transcribe each record. Once the records are verified through an automated validating system, the data is then sent into a database, which is accessible to the public and scientific community. The BPP has had widespread success in recruiting volunteers to revive this historic dataset and prepare it for use by the scientific community.

OMG Earthquake! Can Twitter Improve Earthquake Response
Earle, P., Guy, M., Buckmaster, R., Ostrum, C., Horvath, S., and Vaughan, A., 2010, Seismological Research Letters, v. 81, no. 2, p. 246–251, doi: 10.1785/gssrl.81.2.246.

   Following the 12 May 2008 Wenchuan, China, earthquake, discussion circulated on the Internet describing how the USGS's earthquake notification lagged behind firsthand accounts sent through Twitter, a popular Internet-based service for sending and receiving short text messages referred to as "tweets." A prominent technology blogger, Robert Scoble (*http://scobleizer.com*), is generally credited for being the first to aggregate and redistribute tweets from people in China who directly experienced and reported the shaking resulting from the Wenchuan earthquake.

On the Road Again for a Bird Survey that Counts
Ziolkowski Jr., D., Pardieck, K., and Sauer, J.R., 2010, Birding, v. 42, no. 4, p. 32–41.
https://www.pwrc.usgs.gov/bbs/bbsnews/Pubs/Birding-Article.pdf

   Since its inception in 1966, the Breeding Bird Survey (BBS) has filled a vital role of identifying at-risk bird species for Federal, State, and private entities. The BBS is a scientifically rigorous roadside survey maintained by a highly skilled, largely volunteer workforce of nearly 3,000 observers. As the primary source of large-scale, long-term population data for over 400 of North America's breeding bird species, this collaborative effort between the USGS and the Canadian Wildlife Service is widely recognized as being one of the most efficient large-scale monitoring efforts ever created. Many peer-reviewed articles appear in journals annually in which scientists use the publicly available dataset to evaluate diverse and contemporary topics, such as disease tracking, invasive species research, and climate change. As new analytical methods and spatial technologies emerge, the BBS program continues to affirm its commitment to meeting developing science needs through ongoing growth and improvement of the Survey's core strengths.

Teaching Citizen Science Skills Online: Implications for Invasive Species Training Programs
Newman, G., Crall, A., Laituri, M., Graham, J., Stohlgren, T., Moore, J.C., Kodrich, K., and Holfelder, K.A., 2010, Applied Environmental Education and Communication, v. 9, no. 4, p. 276–286, doi: 10.1080/1533015X.2010.530896.

Citizen science programs are emerging as an efficient way to increase data collection and help monitor invasive species. Effective invasive species monitoring requires rigid data-quality assurances if expensive control efforts are to be guided by volunteer data. To achieve data quality, effective online training is needed to improve field skills and reach large numbers of remote sentinel volunteers critical to early detection and rapid response. The authors evaluated the effectiveness of online static and multimedia tutorials to teach citizen science volunteers (n=54) how to identify invasive plants; establish monitoring plots; measure percent cover; and use Global Positioning System (GPS) units. Participants who were trained using static and multimedia tutorials provided less ($p<.001$) correct species identifications (63 percent and 67 percent) than did professionals (83 percent) across all species, but they did not differ ($p=.125$) between each other. However, their ability to identify conspicuous species was comparable to that of professionals. The variability in percent plant-cover estimates between static (±10 percent) and multimedia (±13 percent) participants did not differ ($p=.86$ and .08, respectively) from those of professionals (±9 percent). Trained volunteers struggled with plot setup and GPS skills. Overall, the online approach used did not influence conferred field skills and abilities. Traditional or multimedia online training augmented with more rigorous, repeated, and hands-on, in-person training in specialized skills required for more difficult tasks will likely improve volunteer abilities, data quality, and overall program effectiveness.

Twitter Earthquake Detection: Earthquake Monitoring in a Social World
Earle, P., Bowden, D.C., and Guy, M., 2011, Annals of Geophysics, v. 54, no. 6, p. 708–715.

The USGS is investigating how the social networking site Twitter, a popular service for sending and receiving short, public text messages, can augment USGS earthquake response products and the delivery of hazard information. Rapid detection and qualitative assessment of shaking events are possible because people begin sending public Twitter messages (tweets) within tens of seconds after feeling shaking. Here we present and evaluate an earthquake detection procedure that relies solely on Twitter data. A tweet-frequency time series constructed from tweets containing the word "earthquake" clearly shows large peaks correlated with the origin times of widely felt events. To identify possible earthquakes, we use a short-term-average, long-term-average algorithm. When tuned to a moderate sensitivity, the detector finds 48 globally distributed earthquakes, with only two false triggers in 5 months of data. The number of detections is small compared to the 5,175 earthquakes in the USGS global earthquake catalog for the same 5-month time period, and no accurate location or magnitude can be assigned based on tweet data alone. However, Twitter earthquake detections are not without merit. The detections are generally caused by widely felt events that are of more immediate interest than those with no human impact. The detections are also fast; about 75 percent occur within 2 minutes of the origin time. This is considerably faster than seismographic detections in poorly instrumented regions of the world. The tweets triggering the detections also provided very short first-impression narratives from people who experienced the shaking.

Vision for a Partnership Between USGS and Our Nation's Schools To Solve Ecological Problems
Pickering, J., 2012, Unpublished material.
http://www.discoverlife.org/usgs/

Let's enable teachers and their students to run a network of ecological research sites around the world, engage them and their communities in science, and generate the knowledge that society needs to understand and address pressing environmental issues.

User-Friendly Web Mapping: Lessons From a Citizen Science Web Site
Newman, G., Zimmerman, D., Crall, A., Laituri, M., Graham, J., and Stapel, L., 2010, International Journal of Geographical Information Science, v. 24, no. 12, p. 1851–1869, doi: 10.1080/13658816.2010.490532.

Citizen science Web sites are emerging as a common way for volunteers to collect and report geographic ecological data. Engaging the public in citizen science is challenging and, when involving online participation, data entry, and map use, becomes even more daunting. Given these new challenges, citizen science Web sites must be easy to use, result in positive overall satisfaction for many different users, support many different tasks, and ensure data quality. To begin reaching these goals, we built a geospatially enabled citizen science Web site, evaluated its usability, and gained experience by working with and listening to citizens using the Web site. We sought to determine general perceptions, discover potential problems, and iteratively improve Web-site features. Although the Web site was rated positive overall, map-based tasks identified a wide range of problems. Given our results, we redesigned the Web site, improved the content, enhanced the ease of use, simplified the map interface, and added features. We discuss citizen science Web sites in relation to online Public Participation Geographic Information Systems (GIS), examine the role(s) Web sites may play in the citizen science research model, discuss how citizen science research advances GIScience, and offer guidelines to improve citizen-based Web mapping applications.

Women in Technology—Maui Economic Development Board
Young, I., 2012, Various materials.
http://www.womenintech.com/

Our mission is to build and strengthen the education to workforce pipeline by encouraging girls, women, and other under-represented groups into Science, Technology, Engineering, and Mathematics careers. The Women in Technology Project is a statewide workforce development initiative of the Maui Economic Development Board, funded in part through grants from the U.S. Departments of Labor, Agriculture, and Education.

Appendix F.   Resources on Volunteer Monitoring

Barb Horn shared many helpful resources, which are publicly available on a Web site (*http://acwi.gov/monitoring/vm/ resources.html*) from the National Water-Quality Monitoring Council (NWQMC). This site offers links to access several mailing lists on volunteer monitoring, newsletters on the topic, as well as survey results, factsheets, and many detailed guides to assist with program development.

Barb presented abbreviated survey results from the Independent Sector, who performs biennial surveys in giving and charitable behavior nationwide. Their findings provide helpful information on motivation of volunteers and are summarized in part here from her slides. More details are included in the Volunteer Management Guide offered by the NWQMC resource page noted above.

- Forty-four percent of adults (21 and older) volunteer for a formal organization.

- Sixty-three percent of those volunteer on a regular basis.

- Thirty-nine percent prefer regular times, weekly, biweekly, monthly vs. 41 percent sporadic, and one-time involvement.

- Women are slightly more likely to volunteer than men.

- Forty-two percent found out about activities through personal contact; 35 percent via participation in an organization.

- Eighty-nine percent volunteered when directly asked by another individual.

- Sixty percent of those who volunteered had Internet access; only 10 percent used it to search for volunteer activities.

- An estimated 83.9 million American adults volunteer, representing the equivalent of over 9 million full-time employees at a value of $239 billion (year 2000 dollar value).

Appendix G.   Citizen Science Projects

Citizen Science projects featured in workshop presentations and working group discussions:
* indicates USGS project
^ indicates a partner project
# indicates external project or historical partner

Alaska Volcano Observatory Citizen Network Ash Collection and Observation Program*
Kristi Wallace, kwallace@usgs.gov
http://www.avo.alaska.edu/ashreport.php
http://www.avo.alaska.edu/ashreports/report_map.php

This program provides simple instructions on how to take a variety of observations about volcanic ash in Alaska: thickness measurements, measured-area sampling, time-incremental sampling, and bulk sampling. It gives people the choice to report what they feel able to do. It is not yet available online.

Boise Watershed Watch ^
Cindy Busche, boisewatershed@cityofboise.org
http://bee.cityofboise.org/watershed/act/watershed-watch!/

Individuals, families, and groups take part in the watershed-wide effort to collect water-quality data along the shores of the Boise River, ponds, reservoirs, and creeks.

Breeding Bird Survey*
Keith Pardieck, kpardieck@usgs.gov
http://www.pwrc.usgs.gov/bbs/

Participants skilled in avian identification collect bird population data along roadside survey routes, following a complex protocol. Over 4,100 survey routes are located across the continental U.S. and Canada. Once analyzed, BBS data provide an index of population abundance that can be used to estimate population trends and relative abundances at various geographic scales. Trend estimates for more than 420 bird species and all raw data are currently available via the BBS Web site.

Butterflies and Moths of North America #
Kelly Lotts, butterflies.moths@gmail.com
http://www.butterfliesandmoths.org

The Butterflies and Moths of North America (BAMONA) project is an ambitious effort to collect and provide access to quality-controlled data about butterflies and moths for the continent of North America from Panama to Canada.

Citizen Science Cattail Monitoring Project ^
Joy Marburger, Joy_Marburger@nps.gov, Beth Middleton, Beth_Middleton@usgs.gov
http://nwrcwebapps.cr.usgs.gov/cattail/

The project aims to inform the public about the changes going on in cattail populations, especially hybridization, that contributes to their invasiveness in wetlands. The goal is to show that cattail spread aggressively and reduce wetland biodiversity. Citizen scientists collect morphological data, habitat conditions, and plant materials that can be used for showing wetland changes across the landscape. Citizens learn about wetlands in various parts of the United States.

Citizen Science Central #
Jennifer Shirk, jls223@cornell.edu
http://www.birds.cornell.edu/citscitoolkit

Citizen science, volunteer monitoring, and participatory action research—this site supports organizers of all initiatives where public participants are involved in scientific research, sharing best practices and ideas among the community.

citsci.org #
Greg Newman, gregory newman@colostate.edu
http://www.citsci.org

This is an online forum where you create your own projects where trained volunteers and scientists together answer local, regional, and global questions; inform natural resource decisions; advance scientific understanding; and improve environmental education. CitSci.org provides tools to empower you and your participants to ask questions, select methods, submit data, analyze data, and share results.

Colorado River Watch ^
Barb Horn, barb.horn@state.co.us
http://wildlife.state.co.us/LandWater/Riverwatch/Pages/Riverwatch.aspx

Associated with the Rocky Mountain Watershed Network, Colorado River Watch trains private and public school teachers and students to collect and analyze samples, providing a hands-on experience for individuals to understand the value and function of the river ecosystem. They collect quality aquatic-ecosystem data over space and time to be used for the Clean Water Act and other water-quality decisionmaking processes.

Cricket Crawl *
Sam Droege, sdroege@usgs.gov
http://www.birds.cornell.edu/citscitoolkit/projects/pwrc/cricketcrawl

The Cricket and Katydid Crawl of New York City (NYC) and Surrounds is a citizen science pilot project in which participants will venture out between dusk and midnight to locations of their choosing throughout the NYC metro area to listen for the calls of crickets and katydids and document their observations.

Did You Feel It? *
David Wald, wald@usgs.gov
http://earthquake.usgs.gov/dyfi

DYFI Web site is intended to tap the abundant information available about earthquakes from the people who actually experience them. By taking advantage of the vast numbers of Internet users, we can get a more complete description of what people experienced, the effects of the earthquake, and the extent of damage than traditional ways of gathering felt information. Best of all, with your help we can do so almost instantly. Not only will you add valuable information on the extent of ground shaking and damage, but in the process we hope you will learn more about how other communities fared and gain a greater understanding of the effects of earthquakes.

Did You See It? *
Rex Baum, baum@usgs.gov
http://landslides.usgs.gov/dysi

Web site and database are used for reporting landslides in order to raise public awareness of landslides and the dangers they pose. We also hope to supplement information that USGS scientists are able to collect about where and when landslides occur. Citizens can submit reports and photographs of landslides through our Web site. Reports are posted to the site.

Discover Life #
John Pickering, pick@discoverlife.org
http://www.discoverlife.org

Discover Life hosts and (or) partners with a series of projects for naturalists, teachers, students, scientists, and others to become involved in research and help investigate the impacts of weather, invasive species, pollution, and other factors on species and their interactions.

Encyclopedia of Life & iNaturalist #
Jennifer Hammock, hammock@si.edu
http://eol.org/info/339

Using the free tools provided by EOL and iNaturalist, approved species lists created on EOL can now be turned into mobile observation checklists on the free iNaturalist iPhone application (app) and the iNaturalist Web site. Observations made through the iPhone app in the field can be shared with the world through iNaturalist, where observations are organized, managed, and posted for others to see.

Hawaii Coqui Crawl *
Derek Masaki, dmasaki@usgs.gov

This project is working to identify locations, model the distribution, and gather information about the general abundance of coqui frogs, house geckos, and native crickets in Hawaii, with input from students and the general public.

iDigBio's Public Participation in Digitizing Museum Specimens #
Austin Mast, amast@bio fsu.edu
https://www.idigbio.org/content/accelerating-scientific-discovery-through-public-participation

This working group engages the public directly and, via crowdsourcing, to centralize and simplify the digitization of museum specimens.

Lake Michigan Volunteer AMBLE: Avian Monitoring for Botulism Lakeshore Events *
Jennifer Chipault, jchipault@usgs.gov
https://www.nwhc.usgs.gov/amble/

This project solicits volunteers to walk the beach of their choice every 7 to 10 days between June and November each year. The contributors receive training on avian botulism detection and reduction and contribute their data to Lake Michigan botulism research via a data entry Web site.

Mid-Winter Bald Eagle Count #
Wade Eakle, Wade.L.Eakle@spd02.usace.army.mil
http://ocid.nacse.org/nbii/eagles/

This project monitors the status of Bald Eagle wintering populations in the contiguous United States by estimating national and regional count trends, overall, and by age class. Each January, several hundred individuals count eagles along standard, nonoverlapping survey routes. It is currently sponsored by the U.S. Army Corps of Engineers.

NWIS Web Services Snapshot Tool for ArcGIS *
Sally Holl, sholl@usgs.gov
http://txpub.usgs.gov/snapshot

The National Water Information System (NWIS) Web Services Snapshot Tool for ArcGIS (Snapshot Tool) gives citizen scientists instant access to the "gold standard" national database of water information, USGS NWIS. The ESRI ArcMap 10.0 add-in is used to retrieve and manage local-scale information about sites, current streamflow, daily streamflow, and water-quality measurements. The Snapshot Tool is an example of how citizen science projects can leverage USGS Water Services (http://waterservices.usgs.gov/) with a custom application. Access the software and VB.NET source code at the Snapshot Tool Web site.

Nature's Notebook, a project of the USA National Phenology Network *
Jake F. Weltzin, jweltzin@usgs.gov
http://www.usanpn.org

The USA National Phenology Network brings together citizen scientists, government agencies, nonprofit groups, educators, and students of all ages to monitor the impacts of climate change on plants and animals in the United States. The network harnesses the power of people and the Internet to collect and share information, providing researchers with far more data than they could collect alone.

NetQuakes *
Lisa Wald, lisa@usgs.gov
http://earthquake.usgs.gov/monitoring/netquakes/

USGS developed a new type of digital seismograph that communicates its data to the USGS via the Internet. The seismographs connect to a local network via WiFi and use existing broadband connections to transmit data after an earthquake. The instruments are designed to be installed in private homes, businesses, public buildings, and schools with an existing broadband connection to the Internet.

Nonindigenous Aquatic Species (NAS) Online Sighting Report System *
Pam Fuller, pam_fuller@usgs.gov, Matt Cannister, mcannister@usgs.gov
http://nas.er.usgs.gov/

This project provides a central repository for spatially referenced biogeographic accounts of nonindigenous aquatic species in the United States. It includes verified occurrences, maps, and species pages for freshwater nonindigenous aquatic animal species. Citizens can report a species via an online reporting form.

North American Amphibian Monitoring Program *
Linda Weir, lweir@usgs.gov
www.pwrc.usgs.gov/naamp

The purpose of the project is to assess population change for frogs and toads. Citizen scientists learn to identify their local frogs and toads by their unique breeding vocalizations and then conduct frog call surveys at predetermined locations along an "adopt a survey" route.

North American Bird Phenology Program *
Jessica Zelt, jzelt@usgs.gov; Sam Droege, sdroege@usgs.gov
http://www.pwrc.usgs.gov/bpp/

This program is part of the USA-National Phenology Network and was a network of volunteer observers who recorded information on first arrival dates, maximum abundance, and departure dates of migratory birds across North America. Active between 1880 and 1970, the program was coordinated by the Federal Government and sponsored by the American Ornithologists' Union. It exists now as a historic collection of 6,000,000 migration card observations, illuminating almost a century of migration patterns and population status of birds. Today, in an innovative project to curate the data and make them publically available, the records are being scanned and placed on the Internet, where volunteers worldwide transcribe these records and add them into a database for analysis.

Public Participation GIS (PPGIS) *
Tim Kern, kernt@usgs.gov
http://my.usgs.gov/ppgis (restricted by login)

This project provides a way for citizens to map areas of concern, as well as discoveries (species observations, habitat disconnects, and disturbance issues) in targeted national forests.

Purple Loosestrife Volunteers ^
Beth Middleton, middletonb@usgs.gov
http://www.nwrc.usgs.gov/special/purplel/index.htm

Volunteers measure the height of Lythrum salicaria in various parts of the world. The data are reported on a Web site and will eventually be a part of a paper to describe the worldwide growth of the species along latitudinal gradients in Eurasia and North America.

Quake Catcher Network *
Elizabeth Cochran, ecochran@usgs.gov
http://qcn.stanford.edu/

This is a collaborative initiative for developing the world's largest, low-cost, strong-motion seismic network by utilizing sensors in and attached to Internet-connected computers.

Social.Water and CrowdHydrology #
Mike Fienen, mnfienen@usgs.gov
http://crowdhydrology.org

Social.Water is an open-source package to collect and parse hydrologic data from text messages. CrowdHydrology is the first project to use Social.Water as an engine, encouraging citizen scientists to send in messages reporting stage at gages equipped with signs on headwater streams.

STEMworks #
Isla Young, isla@medb.org
http://www.sip-hawaii.org/stemworks

Unlike any other class in Hawaii's middle and high school curriculum, STEMworks is a multi-faceted, hands-on program where students get to use the most current, high-end technologies in actual service learning projects. As STEMworks teams work on current community issues, the process teaches them to acquire and analyze information, tackle locally based issues, and apply the latest high-tech solutions.

Student Watershed Research Project #
Mary Ann Schmidt, maryanns@pdx.edu

This is a program to involve high school students in the collection of stream-monitoring data, such as water-quality, biological, and physical data.

The National Map Corps/ Open Streetmap Collaborative Project *
Greg Matthews, gsmatthews@usgs.gov
https://my.usgs.gov/confluence/display/nationalmapcorps/Home

USGS has developed a prototype online editor to allow volunteers to contribute data to *The National Map* and The National Structures Dataset.

USGS Tweet Earthquake Dispatch (TED) *
Paul Earle, pearle@usgs.gov
http://earthquake.usgs.gov/earthquakes/ted/

Via Twitter, this project distributes alerts for earthquakes worldwide with magnitudes of 5.5 and above, including the frequency of tweets in a region surrounding the event that contain the word "earthquake" or its equivalent in several languages, often originating from people who have experienced the shaking effects of the earthquake. After some significant earthquakes, @USGSted will also tweet supplementary information about the event.

Wildlife Health Event Reporter (WHER) #
Megan Hines, wher@wdin.org
http://www.wher.org

Early detection of health events that affect wildlife is often difficult to achieve. There must be observers in the area to take note of the event, and have knowledge of what to do with that information. To help address this need, the Wildlife Data Integration Network (WDIN) developed WHER. People engaging in their regular work or recreational activities have tremendous potential to observe and record events that may identify important changes in the environment. The Wildlife Health Event Reporter is an experimental tool that hopes to harness the power of the many eyes of the public to better detect these changes. WHER is a Web-based application launched to record wildlife observations by citizens concerned about dead or sick wildlife. After being recorded, these observations are joined with other wildlife sightings and are viewable in tabular reports or on a map, enabling people to see where similar events are happening.

Appendix H.   Abbreviations and Glossary

AESIR   Applied Earth Systems Informatics Research

API   application programming interface. An application programming interface provides routines, variables, and classes of technical specifications used for software-to-software communications.

CAD   Computer Aided Design

CBC   Christmas Bird Count

CDI   Community for Data Integration (*https://my.usgs.gov/confluence/display/cdi/Home*)

CIDA   USGS Center for Integrated Data Analytics

CSAS   Core Science Analytics & Synthesis Program

CSS   Core Science Systems mission area

CSWG   Citizen Science Working Group

Data.gov   A Web site to provide public access to high-value, machine-readable datasets generated by the Executive Branch of the U.S. Federal Government.

DMP   data management plan

EOL   Encyclopedia of Life

FOIA   Freedom of Information Act

GIS   geographic information system

HTML5   The 5th revision of the HyperText Markup Language for structuring and presenting content for the World Wide Web, and a core technology of the Internet. Still under development, a major addition of HTML5 is the support of multimedia while still being legible to both humans and computers.

iDigBio   Integrated Digitized Biocollections

iPlover   USGS science project using a handheld application to collect data on Piping Plovers.

NACI   National Agency Check with Inquiries

NAS   USGS Nonindigenous Aquatic Species Program

NAWQA   National Water-Quality Assessment Program

NSF   National Science Foundation

OMB   Office of Management and Budget

OpenID   An open standard that describes how a user can be authenticated for access to a system using credentials (login and password) that are broadly accepted among many different systems.

Open data Structuring and exposing data and information on the Internet so they are: accessible for meaningful use and reuse by anyone through search, download, or other means of access; discoverable by any device; and machine readable.

OSTP   Office of Science and Technology Policy

PIA   privacy impact assessment. Titles II and III of the E-Government Act of 2002 require that agencies evaluate systems that collect personally identifiable information (PII) to determine that the privacy of this information is adequately protected. The mechanism by which agencies perform this assessment is a privacy impact assessment (PIA).

PII   personally identifiable information. The term refers to information that can be used to distinguish or trace an individual's identity, such as their name, social security number, biometric records, and so forth, alone, or when combined with other personal or identifying information, which is linked or linkable to a specific individual, such as date and place of birth, mother's maiden name, and so forth.

PPSR   public participation in scientific research. The involvement of citizen participation in many aspects of scientific research.

PRA   Paperwork Reduction Act. The Paperwork Reduction Act establishes a broad mandate for agencies to perform their information activities in an efficient, effective, and economical manner.

STEM   Science, Technology, Engineering, and Math

TED   USGS Tweet Earthquake Dispatch project

TOS   Terms of service. Rules or conditions that must be agreed upon by a user or an organization before using a service or product.

USGS   U.S. Geological Survey